The High
Southend-on-Sea

Carol Edwards

Copyright Carol Edwards ©
ISBN 978-0-9562201-5-8
Published by Carol Edwards 2016

Acknowledgements

The Raven Family
Phil Wren
Graham Mee
Pat Holden
Sheila Appleton
Margaret Connor
Ray Woodcock
Roy Dilley
Yvonne Lewis

Sources
The Forum and Essex Record Office
My thanks to The Evening Echo for allowing me to use photographs
from the Southend Standard and the Echo Newspapers.

And to all those who allowed me to use family portraits in this book.

To my husband Barry for all his help and technical support and to
Chris for her patience in helping me compile this book and designing
the cover.

Front and back cover copyright to Phil Wren

Contents

Contents (continued)

New Beginnings

To research and document every business or individual that has ever graced the High Street over the decades would be a monumental task requiring a very large book. As Prittlewell developed, people came from all round the country to open shops, coffee houses manage early public houses, which had streets named after them, the Duke of Clarence and the Duchess of York. Doctors, Dentists and Chemists were needed to look after the health of the growing population. Large department stores such as Brightwells, Ravens, Keddies and Dixons, began selling all manner of goods under one roof. It is hard to imagine that at first there was only a butchers and a baker to serve the relatively small number of dwellings around what was to be known as upper South End or Prittlewell. Change came when Daniel Scratton in January 1792 leased land overlooking the Thames, on which was built a hotel and a terrace of houses. Eventually a dirt track would be cleared, running from this new building to the London Road no doubt making it easier for the stagecoach to bring its passengers to their seaside destination. Daniel Robert Scratton (1819-1901) sold off more and more of his land, some of which was to became the High Street. The Scratton story can be viewed today in the museum in Priory Park, where Daniel and his wife once resided

Royal Library at the top of Pier Hill
Essex Record Office

Around the 1790s the Royal Hotel was built overlooking the cliffs and just along the way at the top of Pier Hill (previously known as the Royal Hill) was added the Royal Library (all given a regal title because Princess Caroline once stayed in the nearby terrace). A journal of 1824 noted that *"it has a good reading room and is well supplied with London and provincial papers, periodicals and publications"*. With only the middle to upper classes staying at the resort in the early days, the library provided them with all their reading martial and amusements in the evening. The 1860s saw Mary Woosnam (whose brother became a prominent citizen) as librarian leasing the premises for over 20 years. Charles and Zillah Bullock followed in 1890. Charles also began selling tobacco and stationery as well as providing newspapers for the next few years. The couple managed the Royal Library for eleven years until 1901 when a Receiving Order was made against Zillah Bullock. A sale of the Royal Library in June 1913 together with the adjoining land was sold by auction to Fredrick Ramuz for £4,000 pounds.

High Street

1856 the London Tilbury and Southend Railway finally reached Southend, the company had originally planned to run the track along the seafront, building a station by the pier. A seemingly good idea, as they saw the majority of their travellers being visitors to this up and coming seaside resort. The residents of the prestigious terrace directly above had other ideas and protested long and hard against the thought of having smoke emulating from below and all the noise associated with it. Hence the station is to be found halfway down the High Street with a bridge spanning the street below. Three years after the LTS arrived, a speculator for the sole purpose of providing residential traffic for the railway, planned a new housing estate.

In 1859 Sir Samuel Peto (an investor in the railway) leased fifty acres of land, which at that time was just fields between the railway and the cliffs in Prittlewell, from Daniel Scratton. The housing project would be called "Shorefields". The rent to Daniel Scratton was set first at just a £150 rising to £600 within four years. An elegant shopping parade was added in Nelson Road and was considered the first High Street in Prittlewell, but with increased numbers of potential customers the demand for more and varied shops saw the rapid development of the High Street as we know it today. Peto's desire for only the very best of society living on his estate, led to his bankruptcy, by simply ensuring the train timing allowed only six and half hours to work in the city. The average gentleman traveller needed at least eight to nine hours. So many of the properties remained unsold. It would be years before the train timetable changed, thus promoting the building of vast estates in Westcliff, Prittlewell and beyond for locals and those wishing to travel to the city. By Edwardian times the once single dirt track had become an incredible tide of pedestrians, horse and cart, carriages then trams and motor cars. There were a few individual houses built on the High Street but they were soon swallowed up in the name of progress but the accommodation above the shops still remains today. One area of housing that was not built for the masses was Royal Terrace and although not on the High Street there very presence would have helped fuel the demand for a better shopping experience.

In a prime position overlooking the Thames, the Terrace of Georgian houses attracted only residents with position or money. Rather than the row of buildings being built all at once there appeared to be only four houses in 1848, the widow of a banker, Mrs Dendy at number 4 with a Lady Sharpe at number 5, Major General Tonson living in number

Southend Standard

2

High Street

Southend Standard

6 and a Mrs Bingham occupying number 8. By 1874 there were ten houses standing on top of the cliff. Three were lived in by clergymen, the Reverend Thomas Scott Scratton from Hackney, who when he died in 1887 left £25,000. Also living there was the Reverend Frederick Thackery vicar of Shopland and the Reverend Alfred Oliver Wellstead. Other residents were John Rumble a land owner from Kent, William Gregson an Attorney (he remained here until 1906), Robert Henry Haygate a JP and farmer, and Robert Wright a Stonemason. Other distinguished house owners were John Page a gentleman farmer (a man whose wealth or income allows him to farm for pleasure rather than personally working the land), John Pritchard a successful retired licensed victualler who passed away here in 1887 and a Sir John Wilson. Planning permission was sought twice in 1887, first for three houses to be built and added to the terrace and then George Deeping a retired practitioner submitted plans to the local board to build a property at what would become known as number 19 (he was already living at number 8). The house would be built by a Thomas Whur a local builder of some substance as he employed twenty four men and three boys. John Brightwell owner of a large department store applied to add a greenhouse at his home at number 15 in 1891. The terrace remains today but is mixture of private houses and small hotels.

Although many business that were on the High Street and the section known as the Broadway in the 1950s are long forgotten many of the towns benefactors such as R A Jones and Garons have left a lasting legacy in the development of Southend-on-Sea. Today (2016) the shopping precinct is pedestrianised and where once there was small individual shopkeepers the majority are now part of large corporate groups. Recently small independent greengrocers have opened returning in someway to trading of a bygone age.

The Royal Terrace today (2016)
© B Edwards

3

High Street

A Personal Perspective

Having lived in Southend-on-Sea since 1947, I have, like most long term residents seen a total transformation of the High Street. Although a great number of the shops I remember have gone, such as Woolworths, Dixons, Keddies, Sopers, Garons Cinema, I am pleased to say Marks and Spencers still remains. My earliest memories are as a young teenager being allowed to go shopping with friends on

a Saturday. A bus into town from my home in Westcliff was a real adventure, ending of course at Victoria Circus and the large roundabout. Evenings, when I was older, I would go to Garon's cinema (because it was cheap) with my friend Katie. I am glad to report that we are still friends today. Other memories are of buying my white gloves from Dixons at Victoria Circus, to go with my dress, worn over a heavily starched petticoat and ridiculous winkle picker shoes (naturally at the time I thought I was the bees knees). These shoes – which in this day and age might be classed as lethal weapons – had to

The famous Dome – Kursaal

be handmade at a shoe shop in York Road. Entertainment in those days would have been a dance at the Kursaal or the London Hotel, finishing at the respectable hour of 10.30 or maybe 11pm. In the winter the town died, the seafront, where I spent many a happy hour ceased to be. Those of us resident teenagers, formed a group of boys and girls and hung out at the Capri in Weston Road (just off the high street) Having roared down the

main road, no doubt annoying people the age I am today! I often wondered (as you do when young) who I would marry, but fate gave a helping hand by moving my husband's family from London. We met married and are still together after 52 years. The High Street then took on a whole different meaning.

Author outside Capri 1962

A place to shop together on a Saturday, go out for an evening drink and of course go to the

Barry Edwards 1962 Weston Road

more upmarket cinemas. As the years passed and our daughters were born, the High Street became a refuge for me seeking time alone and a chance to wander round the shops and meet other ladies for afternoon tea.

High Street

Hullbridge Theatre Arts performing Joseph

My biggest challenge with the High Street was the year I was a member of Southend Carnival, we filled the High Street with entertainment (some good others indifferent) the most popular being a local dance school who performed to large crowds and collected money for Southend Carnival Association. For the first time I realised (having to walk up and down its length several times to manage the event) just how long the street was. Such hard work, but made easier by Mike Steptoe, Chris Charles and other volunteers. In time the High Street store would provide the first Saturday job for my younger daughter and as both daughters became old enough, somewhere for them to hang out, meet friends and go to the pubs.

I still enjoy losing myself in the High Street for all its changes, a meal with my husband in the various eateries, buying clothes and other items in the new stores springing up. Like many I too have enjoyed the occasional outing to Lakeside but to be honest for me there is nothing like window shopping in the fresh air. The opportunity of meeting old friends and of course no traffic jams on the short drive home.

The High Street 2016
©B Edwards

High Street today showing old Brightwell Building and Royal Hotel in the distance.
©B Edwards

The Royal Hotel

The Royal Hotel or Capitol as it was known originally has been a prominent feature of South End or Prittlewell since the 1790s. You would imagine that a hotel built on a cliff top with a magnificent view offering good clean air, would be prosperous. Unbelievably it has seen as many lean times as well as successful periods when

the rich and middle class began staying for holidays. With lower South End (Marine Parade) mainly for the working classes wanting to enjoy the pubs and other entertainments, this left the top of Pier Hill for the more refined pursuits of the theatre and library. One of the main problems with researching this venue was finding the rightful owner, as so often an individual named as a proprietor was merely leasing the premises from the actual owner. To keep pace with the history of the hotel has not been easy, but I hope to show here as much of its story as possible.

Built on land originally owned by the Scratton family, they gave a 99 year lease in 1791 to a John Pratt, Mathew Lowdoun, a stone mason and John Watts a carpenter. Having developed the hotel and a few houses along Royal Terrace, they sold the property to a Thomas Holland a brick maker (Thomas was responsible for clearing a path through what was then no more than a field, up to the London Road this in time becoming the High Street). Along with his brothers Samuel and George they obtained a mortgage for £4750 in 1792. Samuel Holland was to die in March 1799 and in 1800 Thomas was declared bankrupt. Single membrane of conveyance of the remainder of a 99 year lease from Michalmas 1791. The Royal Hotel Library and other property in Prittlewell belonging to Thomas Holland bankrupt. His properties consisted of eight houses on Market Street and two houses on the west side of the High Street as well as the Royal Hotel.

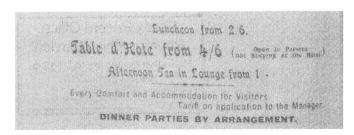

ROYAL HOTEL,
NEW SOUTH-END, ESSEX.

D. MILLER,

Replete with gratitude for the many favours conferred upon him by the Nobility and Gentry, who honoured him with their company last season, takes the earliest opportunities of respectfully informing them, and the Public in general, that his house is fitted up in the most complete manner for their reception, for the present season. The Hotel is extensive, and contains a great variety of sitting and bed-rooms, an elegant assembly-room, and coffee-room, wherein are regularly taken the daily papers. For situation, the Hotel is most happy—commanding from the Terrace, a view of all the shipping passing up and down the River Thames, the shipping in Sheerness Harbour, views of the Isle of Sheppy, Margate, &c.

Posting Machines with proper Guides.

D. Miller has laid in wines of the best vintage, and other liquors of the first quality from the most respectable houses. Dinners dressed and sent out to private houses on the shortest notice, and families served with fine ale and porter.

Excellent stabling, coach-houses, &c. and every travelling accommodation, with post-chaise, &c.

South-End is no more than 42 miles distant from London, from whence a stage-coach arrives every day, from the Blue Bear, Whitechapel.

James Heygate and his wife Anna McMurdo living at Porters, were the owners in 1823 when William Miller was in situ until his death 1827, his widow sold the furniture and the stock in lasted until 1839 with the arrival of Henry Choules and his wife Elizabeth who stayed for seventeen years. Next we find Joseph Robinson as the Licensed Victualler, who according to the Essex Record Office had paid a lump sum and agreed an annual rent of £50 in 1856, to the said owner Elizabeth Anne Heygate (daughter of James) for not only the hotel but the stables behind and number 1 Royal Terrace. Sadly he died just three months later leaving his spinster aunt to become the first female landlord. Already 60 years of age she continued running the establishment until 1870, in her charge were a nephew and niece as well as a large number of staff. James Scott, a widower, previously a successful builder in the town, who had at one time employed fifteen men, took on the Royal Hotel following Maria Browns departure. The number of staff increased during his time to twenty two people, with only one employee, Emma Partridge, who was a local, coming from nearby Leigh-on-Sea. Staff seemed to have more defined roles during his tenure, such as book keeper and head porter. The head waiter, William Tyler, would later marry the widow who owned the London Hotel. During Scott's time the Hotel seemed to be undergoing a period of success, with the accommodation well used by visitors. Staying was Alfred Bellough an architect, William Shaw a ship owner on holiday with his mother, among the other guests were a grain merchant and a barrister. When James Scott died in 1882, he was still resident at the hotel, leaving £20,689 in his will. Benjamin Thomas whose only previous experience had been that of a commercial clerk at a hotel in London, took on the daunting task of the Royal in 1886. With the help of his wife Elizabeth, son and daughter he also employed some fifteen staff. Again we find only the middle to upper class occupying the rooms. A retired army officer, a surveyor and a member of the London Stock Exchange were among their guests. Whilst living here in Southend Benjamin like many local business men was a Mason and was a member of The Priory Lodge. On leaving the area he first managed a small hotel in Kent before going on to be the proprietor of the Albermarie Hotel in Southsea.

With his departure the hotel was next owned by the Southend United Hotel Company, the names of the individual owners unknown, but the company did advertise shares at £10 each. In 1906 Frederick Francis Ramuz paid the company £53,000 pounds for a three year tenancy and a further amount for another three

High Street

Frederick Francis Ramuz

years from the 29th September 1908. He submitted Plans to the council in 1905 to carry out alterations to the building, this caused quite a stir among the townsfolk who thought he meant to alter the main building and character of the establishment. In reality he simply wanted to just extend the existing bar. Frederick Ramuz was one of the more prestigious gentleman to be the proprietor of the Royal. A man of considerable wealth and status he was also involved with the Royal Stores and the Pier Hotel as well as being a Town Councillor and Justice of the Peace, he was also Mayor for two years running in 1896/7. His family were to remain prominent in the town for years after his death in 1946, when he left a staggering £188,724 14s 8d in his will.

1910 saw a Robert James Hannah and his wife Julia taking up residence. The son of a seaman from Hull, his only previous experience had been that of a brewers cashier. The couple stayed at the hotel until 1922 when they returned to Oxford, where his wife had been born. Here they were managers of The Kings Arms until Robert Hannah died in 1927. From 1922–1936 the Webster Brothers owned the hotel but there is little or no information about them. The proprietor after them was a highly experienced licensed victualler who at just 29 years of age had been the manger of The County Hotel, Durham. Harry Cecil Pape (his father was French and the name was originally de-Pape) was born in Manchester in 1872. He married Jane Rose Smith in 1894 and together they managed The Crown Railway Hotel, Rayleigh, Essex, from around 1910–1933 before coming to the seafront at Southend and taking over the Half Way House. Moving on to the Royal in 1937 this was to be their last public house as Jane died soon after leaving Harry to continue alone until his death in 1942.

Southend Standard

The hotel had a mixture of good and indifferent fortune during the 1940s and 50s a Mr C Payne was the manager. In the 1970s there was talk of demolishing the hotel and this prompted the formation of the Southend Area Conservation Group. 1978 Sir John Betjeman paid a visit to the hotel helping to create publicity for those fighting to save it. At the last moment Southend Council stepped in and purchased it from the current owners, Courage Brewery, they then entered into an agreement with Haselmere Estates Ltd to carry out the necessary restoration work. The company were granted a 125 year lease and work was completed in 1980, during the next decade part of the building became a night club. In 2000 the ground floor was converted and became host to popular music nights, but in 2014 the hotel closed when the bailiffs moved in.

Today the hotel is being brought back to life by the Garrett family of Canvey Island. Once again it will be part of Southend's history offering locals and visitors alike, a warm welcome. There will be a restaurant serving a variety of European foods and a cocktail bar, with afternoon tea an option. For the past two hundred years the hotel has had a chequered past but once again there is hope for its future.

Dinner and Dance advert
Courtesy of M Connon

© *B Edwards*

High Street

Royal Stores

The Royal Stores or Tap as it was sometimes known has always had a close connection with The Royal Hotel, often having one landlord or owner at the same time. Sitting on the corner of High Street and Grove Road part of its building looked towards the Thames. But The Royal Stores was nowhere near as prestigious as the Royal Hotel

The earliest record I have been able to find was a Daniel Harrad there from 1845 until his death in 1848. William Claydon born Essex 1818 and his wife Rebecca were the publicans from 1849, running the Store with six servants. On her husband's death in 1869, Rebecca moved to 10 Cliff Parade where for the next thirty years she was a lodging house keeper. For a short period a Charles Cornwall was the Licensed Victualler. Richard Fox took over the tenancy in 1878. From Gravesend in Kent, his second wife Sarah (some twenty eight years younger) was from Essex. Fox was born in Gravesend having five children with his first wife and for ten years was an eating house keeper. Prior to this he had been a bath attendant then a ships steward. For the next eight years until 1886 he managed the Royal Stores with his family, helped by a daughter from his first marriage and a niece. There followed a few years when the Southend Hotel Company and The United Hotel Limited seemed to be running the Tap. In 1906 Frederick Ramuz and an Albert Edward Martin were listed as owners, with a Francis Silvester Baker as the Licensed Victualler from 1910–1926. In 1927 records from Essex Archives showed 23 December conveyance of the Royal Stores or Tap for £12,000 Frederick Francis Ramuz to Mann, Crossman and Paulin Ltd of Albion Brewerey. Also included The Royal Stables and number 3 Grove Road for £15,000. Francis Baker died here in 1948, but not at the Royal Stores, that passed to Harry Hames in 1933.

Incidentals and extras

The following advert appeared in 1871.

Wanted a photographer for the seaside a £1 plus 10%
apply Mr Barrett of the Royal Stores.

1880
Edward Johnson lamp lighter of Southend-on-Sea and Mary Ann Sorrell were charged with stealing a metal tea pot, a cup and saucer and seven knives and forks, their value twelve shillings. All the property of Richard Fox landlord Royal Stores.

1882
The wedding of Christopher Lucking and Miss Berry at St Johns Church saw forty guests supplied with a wedding breakfast at the Royal Hotel. In the evening employees of the railway were provided with a supper at The Royal Stores in honour of the event.

High Street

1883
Sale of The Royal Stores, consisting of a tavern, restaurant with large dinning room (200 persons) smoking room and billiards hall, visited by many excursionists–able to deal with large parties.

1886
A smoking concert took place in the October of this year, the first of the weekly winter season at The Royal Stores. *Concerts with live music for men only, allowing them to smoke and discuss politics.*

1890
Phillip Daniels summoned for keeping open the Royal Stores during prohibited hours The case was dismissed but he was found guilty of allowing his house to be used for gambling.

1892
A cab drivers supper was held on 7th October. The annual dinner took place at the Royal Stores for about fifty people. Mr John Howard presided.

1900s
January 13th Buffalos at Dinner.
A dinner was held at the Royal Stores on Monday to celebrate the 20th Anniversary of the opening of the Royal Great Eastern Lodge. The chair was occupied by "Sir" Lawrence Green, Vice Chair was "Sir" A Bonner. The company numbered fifty. Several new brothers were invested.

1914
Albert Martin submitted plans to Southend Council to make alterations to the Royal Stores.

1914
A plan was submitted by Holmes and Smith to turn a stables into a garage, also put a roof over the yard behind the Royal Stores.

The Stores continued to serve trippers and locals for many years, providing live music at weekends. Like many of the other buildings at that end of the High Street, demolition came in the 1970s to make way for the huge shopping centre known today as The Royals.

The Royal Stores can just be seen to the right of the photograph at the top of Pier Hill opposite the Royal Hotel.

High Street

The British School

There is not much evidence to be found for the exact position of this school. In 1869 Daniel Scratton who was selling off portions of land on and around what is now known as the High Street, mentions the school being built on the corner of a proposed new road, Alexandra Street. In 1890 Frederick Ramuz purchased the plot and converted the building into two shops. We then find Edward Bowmaker as the owner the following year. Bowmaker was originally from Dorset, and was shown in the 1880s as the manager of a coffee house in Alexandra Street. In the 1870s not all children could have an education, only those with money could afford to educate their families. It was said the Quakers founded the British and Foreign Schools for the promotion of Christian knowledge also providing a basic education for the children, but many denominations only offered the poor schooling, if they also attended Sunday school. Reading writing and arithmetic were usually all that was on offer. The British School here in Prittlewell needed funds to carry on its work so in 1872 a leaflet was distributed by the committee of the Southend School, to local residents asking for an annual subscription or donation towards the school's expenses. Always looking for ways to bring in much needed revenue the school made some money by hiring out the main hall and in 1878 an evening of entertainment was held which in the words of the local paper was for "the drinking fund" it reads as if they were collecting money for some sort of jolly. But a lecture was also given that night by friends of the Total Abstinence Society making clear the fund was needed to help those who had fallen victim to the demon drink. The hall was also let weekly to the Southend Philharmonic Society as well as being used for a variety of events throughout the year.

A series of lectures took place in January 1880 the first given by a Miss A E Courtney, who was advertised as the author of a book called "Footsteps in the Snow". Her talk was entitled "The Lights and Shadows of Life". Another quite different occasion was held on the 17th January when a hundred and fifty children sat down to afternoon tea. After refreshments there was a magic lantern show (slide show) to entertain all present. The event was concluded when prizes–books– were presented to some of the children.

16th December 1881 a sale of work and surplice items left over from a fancy goods sale, held back in the summer at the local Congregational Church, was held at the British School. The room was decorated with evergreens and flowers. In the evening there were recitations and glees (songs for three adult voices).

Two of the teachers from 1860 into the 1870s were brother and sister George and Eliza Bigsby from Chelmsford, whose father had been a farmer and able to pay for their education. By 1880 George had the rather prestigious position of Registrar for Births, Deaths and Marriage in the area a post he held until his death in 1907. Leaving his second wife and children well provided for (his first marriage having been childless). By 1890 the school had closed having provided an education for local children for some twenty years.

High Street

Drapers – Tailors – Milliners

Before the advent of modern shopping, online ordering, catalogues delivered to your home, travelling to huge out of town shopping malls you would visit your mainly family run shops on a High Street near where you lived. Southend-on-Sea was no exception below are some of the smaller drapers, gentleman's outfitters, milliners and dressmakers, from the 1850s. Still family run but much larger business were Brightwells, Ravens and Keddies, with Marks and Spencer opening as early as 1914,. British Home Stores came along much later in 1938.

Tailor
Daniel English

The son of an agricultural labourer working the land at Prittlewell, Daniel English was born here in 1830. Quite a leap for a son of a farm labourer to being a tailor, but by 1860 he had married his first wife Eliza Digby and opened a tailors shop on Whitegate Road (later known as High Street). When his wife died in 1888 he had worked on the High Street for over twenty years Following his second marriage he moved to York Street until his death in 1899.

Linen Draper
James Gunn Payne

1851 James Gunn Payne, born in Suffolk 1820, was a linen draper on Milton Street, later moving to number 12 High Street until the 1870s. There were six children born to James and his wife Sarah during their time at Prittlewell.

Draper
Joseph Packham

43 High Street, was where Joseph Packham, in his early twenties, opened a drapers shop. Born in Sussex 1857, he moved here in the late 1870s, later marrying one of his draper's assistants, Annie Woodley in 1881. Their first two children were born here, but by 1884 they had moved back to Josephs home town where he continued as a draper.

Draper
Henry Gallopine Stevenson

Arriving here in the 1870s Henry Stevenson born 1824 in Buckinghamshire, had a varied career. 1861 had seen him as a railway cashier, before moving to Essex, first opening a tea garden 1870s (not on High Street) then 10 years with his drapers shop at number 20 High Street through the 1880s.

Milliner

Jennie Ford had a milliners shop in the 1900s at 136 High Street, but her stay was short. Born in Devon 1862, sharing the premises with her was Mary Dalrymple from London, also a milliner, with young Annie Bass as their assistant.

General & Fancy Draper and Milliner
Ernest Weedon

The son of a commercial traveller, Ernest Weedon was born in Middlesex 1876. A drapers assistant, before coming to Southend where he opened his own shop at 118

ERNEST W. WEEDEN,

NEW GOODS IN ALL DEPART-MENTS.

General & Fancy Draper and Milliner,

118 HIGH STREET, SOUTHEND-ON-SEA.

RELIABLE QUALITIES AT LOW PRICES.

High Street, in 1908. He married Florence Pierson in 1905 and their son Henry was born here in 1909. They were in business on the High Street until 1911, but moved away soon after, Ernest died in 1915, having returned to Middlesex.

Milliner Costumer and Fancy Draper
Robert Payn

With his father a draper and mother a milliner, it was not surprising that Robert Payn followed in their footsteps. First as an apprentice draper in Canterbury, then a linen warehouseman in the 1880s, finally a position as manager of a drapers shop in London in the 1890. Marrying in 1880 Robert and his wife Ellen would have three daughters and one son before moving to Southend in the late 1890s. Their first shop was on Cliff Town Road but later there would be another drapers opened at Tower Buildings, number 75 High Street. Robert Payn and his family were to remain here until his death in Thorpe Bay in 1936.

Mantles: A gas mantle was a small flat fabric mesh bag impregnated with a metal salt. When fitted over a gas burner the bag inflated to spread light.

ROBERT PAYN,

MILLINER....
COSTUMIER,
AND FANCY
DRAPER.

TOWER BUILDINGS,
75 HIGH STREET,
AND
1 CLIFF TOWN RD.

For Mantles, Costumes and Blouses.

The Original Exclusive Mantle Warehouse in Southend. . . .

Still retaining its reputation for Good Wearing Garments at Moderate Prices.

And at London House, 13 Cliff Town Road,

SOUTHEND-ON-SEA.

TELEPHONE, 1675, SOUTHEND.

Terminus House

FRED SQUIER

Has always the very Latest in

**Gent's Neckwear.   Shirts for all occasions.
Hats and Caps.**

SPECIAL VALUE IN LINEN COLLARS,
—— Best Finish and Easy Fitting, 5½d. ——

His father, also Frederick, was a dealer in woollen goods in Surrey where Frederic Jnr was born in 1872. Before coming to Southend-on-Sea, Frederick had a shop as a hat, hosier and shirt maker in London. His first daughter Jessie was born in Lambeth in 1900, but his second daughter Elsie was born here in 1904. His business was sited in Terminus House at 141–143 High Street and was there through the 1920s. Hamlet Court Road Westcliff which was quite a prestigious road, saw his second shop open there in the 1930s. Serving as a JP Frederick Squires remained here until he passed away in 1964.

FRED SQUIER,
TERMINUS HOUSE, *NEAR TRAM TERMINUS* SOUTHEND,
HAS A
Magnificent
Selection
OF
SUITS
IN THE.
One of the
Neatest
of Styles
for . . .
BOYS
from 2 to 6 years,
5/11 to 25/-

FRED SQUIER,
TERMINUS HOUSE, *NEAR TRAM TERMINUS* SOUTHEND,
FOR
HARD WEAR
TWEED
**SUFFOLK
SUITS**
9/11 to 35/-
**NORFOLK
SUITS**
Same shape, made to
button to neck,
From **4/11**
Also is the
Celebrated
Nore Serges
Guaranteed to stand
any hard use.
From **8/11**

He installed an electric lift in his drapers in 1922.

The Interior of the shop

Draper Hatter and Hosier
William Chignall's (father and son)

The first William Chignall (b 1837) was a draper on Grove Road in the 1800s, where his father before him had been a licensed victualler. Becoming a draper on the High Street at number 6, fell to his son William (b1861) who was born here like his father. A hatter and hosier for only a few years between 1890 and 1901.

Men's Clothier
Charles Burley Sayer

BEST VALUE

Men's Clothing

TO MEASURE,

HOSIERY.
HATS.
TIES,
GLOVES.

CHAS. B. SAYER,
45 High Street
(OPPOSITE YORK ROAD).

Son of a journeyman tailor, Charles Sayer was a shop assistant in a gentleman's outfitters in Kent when just 15 years old. Born in Canterbury 1866, Charles moved to Southend where he opened a shop at 45 High Street. In 1890 he had met and married his first wife Susie Katie Heath. Unfortunately eight months after the birth of their son Leonard in 1891, Susie died, leaving £200 in her will. Charles married again in 1894 to a Clara Bowerman and was still to be found on the High Street in the 1900s.

Edwin Smith had a business on the High Street in the 1900s. He was born in Wilshire 1866. In the 1920s there was to be found **Hepworth and Sons** at 106 High Street, **Saxon Outfitters** at 112 with costumier **Henry Proctor** at number 48. The High Street in the 1940s/50s still had many small individual shops, **Rosenberg's** the tailor 165–167, **Greens Costumier** 173–175 and Jennings also a tailor at 193–195. A children's outfitter was at 163 and **Brandons** progressive tailor (whatever that entailed) had a shop at 128. Westwoods Ltd mens outfitter, **Meakers** outfitters 164, Joseph George Buxton, tailor 102. **C Birn and Son Ltd** shirt specialists, exclusive men's wear at 21 High Street **Herbert Leng** at 95 Broadway (High Street) classed himself as a Merchant Tailor

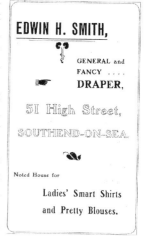

EDWIN H. SMITH,

GENERAL and
FANCY . . . .
DRAPER,

51 High Street,

SOUTHEND-ON-SEA.

Noted House for

Ladies' Smart Shirts
and Pretty Blouses.

H. W. PROCTER & CO.
48 HIGH STREET

Outsize Specialist

Agents for AQUATITE RAINCOATS

BIRN

SHIRTMAKER AND HOSIER

BIRNSONA

EXTENSIVE READY-TO-WEAR DEPT.

AGENT FOR:

21 HIGH STREET - SOUTHEND-ON-SEA

William Heddle
1847 – 1948

Moving to Witham, Essex from Orkney in Scotland where he was born in 1847 he married a Mary Ann Collins in 1870. The couple settled at 32 Park Street, Prittlewell, a ten minute walk from the High Street and opened a drapers shop. Mary was to die in 1878, leaving William with three young children, but in 1880 he married again to one Emma Collins (a coincidence or family member?) some fifteen years younger than himself. The couple simply moved into Park Street and this happy union would in time produce ten children, including James who would be a local Justice of the Peace. Later they would live in Victoria Avenue and

THE SOUTHEND CASH CLOTHING STORES

Proprietor · · · WILLIAM HEDDLE, Junr.

EVERYTHING IN MEN'S & BOYS' WEAR.

HOSIERS and HATTERS.

MEN'S AND BOYS' Ready-to-Wear CLOTHING.

TAILORING
Of a Smart and Dependable STANDARD.

OVERALLS FOR ALL TRADES.

80 HIGH STREET,
SOUTHEND-ON-SEA.

Phone—MARINE 67702. Established 1889.

THE SOUTHEND

CASH CLOTHING STORES

Proprietor: WILLIAM HEDDLE

Specialists
in

MEN'S & BOYS'
SUITS
SPORTSWEAR
RAINCOATS
OVERCOATS
HATS & CAPS
SHIRTS
HOSIERY
and
OVERALLS

GENTLEMANLY
TAILORING
AT
CONSISTENT
PRICES

**80 HIGH STREET
SOUTHEND-ON-SEA**

Phone: SOUTHEND 2677   Established 1889

Warrior Square eventually moving the store to the more prestigious address 80 High Street. 1940 saw the couples Diamond Wedding celebration at Garons Banqueting Hall when William was 93 years old. He died in 1948 at his home 59 Warrior Square, aged 101 leaving £30,525 2s 4d in his will.

Being a draper and outfitter played its part in some of his children's lives, daughters Edna, Rosa and Ethel married drapers. Sons Cyril (Kent) Oscar (Colchester) opened their own business with James being the manager for the family shop on Park Street.

High Street

Sopers

Arthur Soper born in Hampshire in 1871 was the son of a grocer. 1891 saw him working as a drapers assistant in

Southampton, he later secured a position in West Ham. Soon after marrying Rosa Brown in 1898 the couple moved to 114 High Street followed by the birth of their son Arthur in 1899 and their daughter Irene in 1900. When only nine years old Arthur was to die. They were to have two more sons, Kenneth 1907 and Donald in 1910 and a daughter Vera in 1905. Although Sopers was still open in the1950s I am unclear if the sons continued the drapers or the business was sold, the new owners keeping the name.

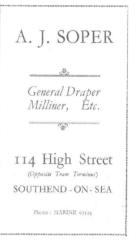

A. J. SOPER

General Draper
Milliner, Etc.

114 High Street
(Opposite Tram Terminus)

SOUTHEND - ON - SEA

Phone: MARINE 67329

Millets

Millets has had a chequered history, with a number of takeovers in its not too distant past. Original business was opened in the 1900s by a draper called Israel Marcus Millett born in Austria in 1867. Opening two shops, one in Southampton the other in Bristol, he was eventually to pass on the Bristol shop to Joseph Spielman, who married his daughter Florence.

Mrs Stokes and Mabel Arnold © R Arnold

Joseph did much to improve on the original merchandise, offering a greater range of clothing and boots. Today Milletts is well known for its outdoor range of jackets, boots, rucksacks and tenting equipment. In the 1940s Mabel Arnold worked for the company and remembered the day when a hit and run German fighter flew down the High Street, the rear gunner shooting up the street, taking out all the windows of the bakers opposite. Today Milletts can still be found just of the High Street in York Road.

MILLETT'S STORES
(1928) LTD.
offer the best value for
CAMPING, HIKING AND OUTDOOR EQUIPMENT

HOLDALLS 18/11 each

CYCLING WEAR

41 HIGH STREET, SOUTHEND Phone 3152

Shoemakers

The world of shoes has changed vastly over the decades. Shoemakers in the early 1700s were a very localised product, with the shoemaker a member of a small community, much like the blacksmith. Shoes were first only made to order, then it became a growth industry with mass production, practically in Northhampton. On Southend High Street like many others around the country, shoemakers worked from home or opened individual shops. I can remember going to a shoemakers in York Road, in the late 1950s, to have my very own winklepickers designed. Today rather than individual shoe emporiums we started to buy our shoes from chains, like Freeman Hardy Willis, Dolcus, Lily and Skinner. But Today we can purchase our footwear from catalogues visit large department stores or if very rich shop at exclusive boutiques selling very expensive brand name shoes. Here are just a few of the boot/shoemakers who were on Southend High Street.

Henry Charles Savage
1848-1935

The son of a journeyman shoemaker (someone who has served an apprenticeship) Charles Savage was born in Norfolk in 1848. Moving to London, he married Mary Ann Campion in 1870 and they had five sons before coming down to Southend where their only daughter was born in 1880. Living first in Hamlet Road, then Cambridge Road, he signed a lease in 1877 for number 11 High Street (re-numbered later as 62) for £60 a year. Two years later another lease on the property for ten years, was to cost £100. For the next 30 years Henry Savage and Sons were boot and shoemakers at number 62.

William Bugg
1817-1901

Originally from Colchester, William Bugg was listed as a cordwainer (one who makes shoes from new leather) like his father before him. He only spent a short time on the High Street occupying number 9 in 1861. His son William later became a ticket collector on the pier.

Lovell Warren
1857-1927

Called The Golden Boot Company Lovell Warren had a large shop on the High Street and another in London. Born 1857 in Shoreditch his father also Lovell was a boot and shoe manufacturer from Northampton. Marrying in Chelmsford in 1885 to Susannah Brown the couple set up home and shop in 1900, staying some 20 years.

JENNINGS'
SHOES

Cheapest and
Best to Buy.

FASHION SHOES
FOR LADIES. All
Styles.

From 18/9

Special Agents for
"BECTIVE,"
"LOTUS,"
"DELTA,"
"JAEGER."

WEST-END MODELS
FOR MEN.

From 21/9

Note 3 Shops.

NELSON ST., CLIFF TOWN, SOUTHEND.
THE BROADWAY, SOUTHEND.
HAMLET COURT ROAD, WESTCLIFF.

From the 1920s buying shoes or boots became more of an industry, with companies having stores all over the country to sell their footwear. The individual shoemaker was gradually disappearing, but the cobbler remained for those wanting shoes repaired. Springing up were multi nationals or limited companies such as the British Shoe Company (no 74), Hilton and Sons Ltd (no 102), J F Tanner Ltd (no 1930), J Sears (no 88) part of the True Form Boot Co. The 1940s saw Dolcis Shoes, Lilly and Skinner and Freeman Hardy Willis.

Freeman Hardy and Willis

The company was originally founded by an Edward Wood in the 1870s, but was purchased by three employees named Freeman, Hardy and Willis. On being bought out by Sears PLC in the 1920s. They removed the "and" so the name would fit better above a shop front. Freeman Hardy Willis had a shop in the town as early as the 1890s.

George Bell - Manager
1892

He was charged with the embezzlement of 18s 6d and a further count of stealing £1 12s 5d from his employers. Having lost his job he blamed drink for his downfall and received two months hard labour. But far from learning a lesson he was arrested again in 1893 for obtaining goods under false pretences.

In the 1890s William Bright a labourer and his wife Hannah were charged with stealing a pair of boots from FHW. The husband pleaded not guilty but his wife admitted the offence. Both were found guilty and received fourteen days hard labour.

A letter from Yvonne Lewis gave me an insight into her young life in Southend when her father was the manager of Freeman Hardy Willis at the bottom end of the High Street.

Like many men Cecil Brame Crossley served in the army during the war, returning home on demob he also resumed his employment with Freeman Hardy Willis, before promotion meant a move with his family to a shop in Grays. In time ending up as the manager of one of their Southend stores. Yvonne recalled, "we lived above the shop and I loved looking out of my bedroom window at the trippers below coming from the railway station, streaming down the street towards the seafront. I lived my young life on Southend High Street, witnessing all the changes. There used to be Hinds the Jewellers,

Eva and Cecil Crossley
© Y Lewis

Mac Fisheries ,Garons, Dunns the men's shop and the Singer Sewing Machine Company". Yvonne worked in the shop prior to marriage in 1958, returning in the 1960s after the birth of her daughter. Cecil Crossley and his wife Eva May lived above the shop until 1966 when they purchased a house, but Cecil continued to be the manager of the shoe shop until his death in 1969.

The shop front in the 1950s
© R Dilley

High Street

Charles Woosnam
1815- 1906

Charles Woosnam
Permission of F
Scantleburey

If ever there was a self made man, it was one Charles Woosnam. Born in Hackney in 1815, we find at the young age of just 23 in 1838, he was the hotel keeper of The Ship Hotel on the seafront. Living with him was his mother Ann. Southend of course was beginning to grow and attract vast numbers of visitors to take the waters, or simply enjoy the fresh air, eat, drink and enjoy themselves. By 1848 Charles was the owner of bathing machines, needed by those who wanted to undress and enjoy a swim, it was a very lucrative way of earning money. Marrying in 1849 he continued running The Ship until the 1850s before moving to 18 High Street, where he was listed as a wine merchant and still owner of The Ship. His involvement with the towns development was shown as early as 1854, when Mr Warick called a meeting on January 27th of that year, in what was then known as the Hope Tavern now Hotel. Having invited may prominent gentlemen of the day including Charles Woosnam, he proposed the need for gas lighting in Southend. At the meeting Woosnam put forward a resolution that they form a gas company with a capital of £1,500 in 300 shares of £5 each. Daniel Scratton land owner of much of the area, donated four acres of land around Royal Terrace, Grove Terrace and the church of St Johns to allow the laying of pipes. May 1855 saw the lighting of 120 gas lamps. It is perhaps interesting to note that young Charles Woosnam had already made sufficient money in order to donate to the scheme.

Charles and Annie Woosnam had seven children living with them at their High Street address along with his mother Ann and his sister Mary, who for 14 years leased the Royal Library (opposite Royal Hotel). Charles was an astute businessman and invested in quite a lot of land on the High Street, which his sons would sell off following his death. Still having retained control of The Ship, in 1873 William Trigg (already a Licensed Victualler) leased the public house, complete with skittle alley for seventeen and a half years at the rent of £65 per annum. By 1883 he arranged for Trigg to purchase exclusively from him all wines and spirits needed for his establishment. To this end his wine merchants served the residents of the town and provided "booze" for the ever increasing numbers of visitors to lower Southend.

During his long life here, Charles Woosnam was a pillar of respectability, serving as a Borough Magistrate. Of his four sons only Charles Junior and John, were wine agents. John moved to Devon, Charles took up residence here in Cambridge Road, where he died in 1928 leaving £10,044 11s in his will. Richard moved to Brentwood, where he had a milk sterilisation and bottling company. Arthur a patent agent moved to Great Warley. Charles Woosnam senior died in 1906.

High Street

William Alfred Lodder
1843 – 1911

A well known clock and watchmaker, William Alfred Lodder was the son of a Licensed Victualler from Hampshire, where he was born in 1843. Aged 14 he was an apprentice watchmaker in his hometown, but by the early 1870s was to be found working at a jewellers in Wales. Married by 1873 and a father to Albert Edward in 1876, who was born here in Southend after his father had set up a shop at 40 High Street.

His business remained at this address for nearly thirty years before moving to Weston Road. One of his apprentices was a Charles G Dowsett, whose father William was a draper in the town, brother to the more famous member of the family – Thomas Dowsett.

When his wife Mary died in 1905 he was still producing his unique clocks as seen in the photo. Living with his son Albert, an iron mongers clerk, William Alfred Lodder died in 1911. His son married in 1913 in London but returned to Prittlewell where his daughter Ruby was born in 1914. However the family did not stay here but eventually moved away to Hertfordshire.

Manager and Owner
Joseph Habgood

Born in Inkpen Berkshire 1853, Joseph Habgood was by 1911 a hatter and hosier at 145 Broadway (also know as High Street). His father was a wheelwright. Marrying Caroline Meridith in 1882, the couple were to be childless. In the 1890s he came to work as a drapers assistant at Brightwells, later becoming manager. His shop was on Southend High Street until his death 1922.

High Street Early 1900s
© Permission of Evening Echo

Arthur Herbert Smith

Arthur Herbert Smith's bakery (store now occupied by Waterstones), was first established in the High Street around 1900, at number 39, where it was to serve among other things stone milled bread, American iced drinks and ices. Home was number 31 High Street. Born in 1862 in Trowbridge, Wiltshire he chose not to follow his father's profession of carpenter and joiner, instead choosing to become a baker. 1881 still found him in Wiltshire learning his trade but by 1893 he had married Ellen Frewin and established his own business. It is perhaps surprising to find that of the seven people he employed only two were what could be classed as locals coming from nearby Paglesham. Alice Waterfield his bookkeeper was from Nottinghamshire, William Martin his assistant baker from Berkshire and the remaining three shop assistants coming from Kent, Chelmsford and Wiltshire. Arthur Herbert Smith was to die in 1917 leaving £32,849 11s 7d to his widow. A very successful baker indeed.

The building today 2016 is now home to
Waterstones book store
© B Edwards

24

High Street

Reginald Percy Frith
1866–1955

Born in 1866, Reginald Percy Frith, always known as Percy, was the son of the

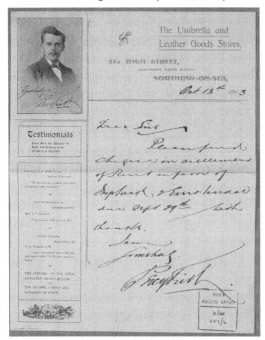

Essex Record Office

Reverend William Frith a non conformist minister of the Trinity Martyr's Church in Kent, where Percy began his life. There were four other children, three brothers and a sister. How or why Percy Frith came to Essex and became first a leather dealer then umbrella maker with a shop at 37a High Street is largely unknown. In 1895 he married Helena Beatse here in Southend-on-Sea. Her mother Mary was a lodging house keeper and it is entirely possible that Percy was lodging with them. The couple went on to have two children, Reginald William 1897 and Frances May 1904, who died unmarried in Devon 1993. Percy was still to be found on the 1911 census manufacturing what was the modern umbrella, with steel ribs and vastly improved waterproofing. The umbrella was still used by ladies as protection against the sun if they didn't possess a parasol.

Like many families in Essex the First World War interrupted their lives, often with devastating consequences. Lieutenant Reginald William Frith died of wounds in a Kingston-upon-Thames hospital in 1918. Percy was among the more fortunate, that his son was returned home when wounded, enabled him to be buried in Leigh Cemetery in the London Road when he passed away. Small comfort, one that was denied to millions.

Helena Frith passed away in 1937, the following year Percy married Leila Canning. By the 1950s they were running a shop on the London Road selling baby carriages. Reginald Percy Frith died in 1955 at the grand age of 89, leaving £424. 9s in his will.

William John Foot
Watchmaker and Art Connoisseur

W. FOOT,
THE PRACTICAL
Watchmaker & Jeweller,
44 HIGH STREET,
SOUTHEND-ON-SEA.

Local Souvenirs in Cups, Spoons, &c., with Borough Arms, in real enamel at 1/6 each.

☞ Picture Lovers should visit the "Leighton Gallery" at same address. Admission Free.

His father was a shipsmith in Southampton where William John Foot was born in 1870. Leaving Hampshire for London, he met and married Ethel Tancok in 1895, and had two daughters, Audrey in London 1897, Hilda after his move to Southend-on-Sea 1901. Living in Queens Road, he worked from home as a watchmaker, later acquiring a shop at 44 High Street, where he not only sold jewellery but opened the Leighton Art Gallery named after the painter Lord Leighton. In 1911 local archaeologists having dug up two thirteenth century wooden figures from Prittlewell Priory and also an old sundial from Sutton Hall Rochford, had the objects displayed at William Foots gallery. Also on show was the late George Tipper's (a local restaurateur) Crimean Medals and a silver teapot formally belonging to Queen Anne. On the walls were displayed many different kinds of paintings by various artists.

William John Foot died here in 1946, his daughter Audrey remained in the town until she passed away in 1986.

The gallery was named after Lord Leighton and was an added attraction to William Foot's jewellery shop. Local Archaeology was not neglected for two 13th century figures dug up at Prittlewell Priory and an old sundial from Sutton Hall were also displayed.

Health Care

Before free health care, people depended on the local chemist (if they could afford it) to offer advice and supply drugs to cure all ills or consulted their Doctor again if having enough money. Just a few of the chemists who were serving the community.

George Robert Dawson
1847 - 1927

A chemist, druggist and a keen photographer George Dawson was one of the first of many shops to sell film for cameras. His first chemists was on Marine Parade when he took over the business of Charles Montague King. George Dawson was born in Sheffield Yorkshire in 1874 and was the son of a music seller! At 14 he was apprenticed to a chemist in his home town. By the early 1870s he was here in Prittlewell managing his own chemist on what was then next to private dwellings and public houses. 1874 came the move to 16 High Street, later he was to establish himself at number 42 from the 1900s until his death there in 1927. George Dawson married twice, his first wife (died) was Kate Parker, they were married in 1879 and had four children, two sons and two daughters. His son George in the 1900s, managed the chemists on Marine Parade, before the world of slot machines took over. Marriage to Eleanor Stevens was in 1909 and lasted till his death.

DAWSON, Chemist and Photographic Dealer,
42 HIGH STREET & 46 MARINE PARADE,
SOUTHEND-ON-SEA.

Life was not without its mishaps for one Sunday in 1912, out on his motorbike with son Robert, they were a few yards from their home when the steering failed, crashing in the side of a cab, both were thrown off into the road. Miraculously neither were injured.

In the 1890s on a busy bank holiday an excursionist accidentally fell down the cliffs and broke her arm in two places. Having been taken to Dawson's chemist shop, Doctor Jones who had a practise nearby was called and set the poor woman's arm. One could not imagine such an incident taking place in the local chemist today.

High Street

George H M King

The son of Charles Montague King, born at Leigh-on-Sea, who for a number of years had a chemist shop on Marine Parade, with a young George as an assistant. By 1890 George had his own premises at number 10 High Street were he was a doctors assistant as well as a chemist, George Herbert Montague King, remained on the High Street until dying in 1916.

Body's

Body's was first a chemist at Westcliff-on-Sea before moving to 167 High Street where the shop was a prominent fixture for a number of years up to the 1950s. Why the move to Westcliff-on-Sea all the way from Devon, after his marriage, is unknown but he kept his original shop even after he opened his chemist in Southend High Street. Sidney Francis Body was born in America in 1882, his arrival in England around 1890, first saw him working as a chemist in Sussex. Later moving to Devon he met his future wife, May Lambshead, who was the daughter of a grocer. Having married in 1908 they moved to Westcliff where in 1910 their son Leslie Charles was born. The family didn't remain in Essex, son Leslie moved to Kent and Sidney Body died in Sussex in 1966.

Boots

The most famous and still prominent chemist on the High Street is Boots. Today occupying a space in the Royals but previously at 130 High Street, now a clothing outlet, the architecture of a bygone age still evident on the upper floor. There cannot be many who have not visited this shop, with outlets all over the country, including two others, one in Hamlet Court Road, Westcliff-on-Sea, the other on the Broadway, Leigh-on-Sea. The chain was founded in the 1840s in Nottinghamshire by John Boot, a medical botanist, who had died by 1860, leaving his wife Mary and son Jesse to carry on his work. The 1881 census showed that his occupation was that of a patient medicine chemist with his wife and sister Jane assisting. Knowing that the vast majority of the population were unable to afford medicine, Jessie Boot formed his business into a modern pharmacy in 1884 and began buying drugs direct from the manufacturer, to keep prices low. Success followed and the company opened Boots  the chemist across the country and employing its own scientists to manufacture drugs. In the 1950s they developed the anti-inflammatory drug Ibuprofen. With his wife Florence born on Jersey, they would have three children, John, Margery and Dorothy. Sir Jesse Boot as he became known died in 1937 but his dream lived on.

Today there are many cut price shops, selling cosmetics, toiletries and the like previously stocked by the old fashioned chemist, but only the odd one or two have a resident chemist to provide medicines on a doctors prescription.

High Street

Doctors

Physicians

Warrick- Deepng and Phillips are perhaps one of the earliest group practices there was to be found in the 1880s. Their practise in Prospect House (now demolished) opposite the Royal Hotel was the home of William Warrick who had been the Doctor in residence since the 1840s.

William Warrick

Born 1818 in Nottinghamshire we know he was here from 1840, because of his marriage to Ann Miller. Practising at first on Marine Parade the move to the more prestigious address- Prospect House at the bottom of the high street came in the 1850s. His daughter Marriane (b 1844) was to marry one George Deeping who joined her fathers practise. In 1881 William was living in Sussex, but when he died in 1892 it was here at Southend on sea.

Edward English Phillips

A physician and surgeon, born in Somerset 1844, the son of a Doctor, he only remained in the town for a few years marrying Emily Swaine in 1879, their daughter Evelyn was born here in 1880. Moving to Bath in the late 1880s son William was born in 1894, by 1901 Edward was retired. He died in Bath in 1925. He left an estate of over £22,000

George Davidson Deeping

From Lincolnshire born in 1848, George Deeping began his medical career at Guys hospital in London in the early 1870s, before moving on to Southend to take up a position as a physician in Prospect House, with Doctor Warrick. He met and married one of his daughters – Marriane. Their first child George Warrick Deeping was born at Prospect House in 1877 (he went on to became a prolific writer) two daughters followed, one died at birth. Retiring in the 1900s to Sussex, he died there in 1909.

General Practitioner

George Francis Jones born in London 1845 was a member of the Royal College of Surgeons – like his father. Although George was born in London, the family moved to Prittlewell in 1846, where all his siblings were born. His father had a practice around the town for many years but when George Francis qualified he took up residence at number 35 High Street with his wife in 1869 (the first of his five sons were born in 1871) also making this address his general practice office where he stayed for over 30 years. Retired by 1911 and living on Westcliff Parade, he died in 1925.

Dental Surgeon

E H Richards

From 1914 Richards was at 124 High Street, later moving the dental surgery moved to Warrior Square in the 1920s where it remained until the 1940s.

ARTIFICIAL A SET, £1 1s. to £10 10s.

TEETH Single Teeth, 2/6 to 21/-

REPAIRS. MISFITS RE-MODELLED.
EXTRACTION, 1/- STOPPING from 2/6.

PAINLESS EXTRACTION - 2/6
No charge when new teeth are supplied.
—— CONSULTATION FREE. ——

Harry Radian

Harry Radian from Shoreditch (b.1898) was the son of Russian parents who came to England in the 1800s. His father was a humble shop fitter but Harry became a pioneer in using hypnosis to extract teeth when giving treatment. Marrying in 1924 he already had a practice upstairs at number 95 High Street. 1942 Radian was taken to Southend Police Court and fined a total of £300 with £21 costs, for the misuse of petrol. An enormous amount of money in those days. This brush with the law did little to harm Harry Radian's reputation as a dentist, by 1950 he had moved to a more salubrious address in Chalkwell Avenue. When he died in 1988 he left a staggering £354,806.

Mary Arnold one of his employees, was unable to be hypnotised as she was particularly strong willed. She recalled the lady newspaper seller, who used to set up her chair on the pavement below, sounding like Deanne Durban when selling her newspapers.

Edwin Arthur Holloway

Born in Northampton in 1852, he was first a chemist then a dental anaesthetist, married twice his eldest son from his first marriage became a dentist then his son Norman from his second marriage a dental surgeon. Moving to Southend-on-Sea with his second wife Bertha he took up residence at 140 Broadway (High Street) by 1911, which first served as home and business address. When he died in 1924 he was living in Thorpe Bay. His son Norman remained in the area passing away in 1980.

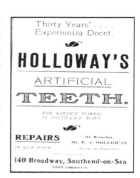

Thomas Dowsett
1838–1906

A field boy (someone who scares birds from a field) to Mayor of Southend-on-Sea, Thomas Dowsett can trace his linage back to his grandfather John Dowsett, born here in 1753. He married Rachell Fitch in 1788, having several children including James 1799, father to the well known Thomas Dowsett. James had married in 1820 to Martha Ingram from nearby Leigh-on-Sea. James was a boot maker all his life in Prittlewell, living on East Street where he died in 1875.

High Street and Beyond

Thomas Dowsett was born in Prittlewell around 1838 and in 1857 at the age of just 19, he married his first wife, Eliza Ann Bradley. Married life began on Marine Parade, Southend, where he was listed as a hairdresser/barber and purveyor of perfume. At one time other shop keepers said that he needed to open his business on a Sunday, if he was to succeed. Dowsett being a practising Christian refused. He had joined the Congregational Body (Protestant) who worshiped in a room belonging to The British School on the High Street. He became one of their original Deacons and introduced Sunday school. Far from not succeeding with his ventures on the seafront and beyond he would in time go on to make his fame and fortune in the town. As early as 1874 he was in partnership with a Thomas Thipthorpe, a builder and Dowsett was listed as a fancy warehouse keeper. Included in the records of the Southend Essex Equitable Investments and Advance Co. Ltd it was noted we are told that Thomas Dowsett and Thomas Thipthorpe already have two loans, one of £2,050 *and £900, secured against property in Southend.* Thomas Dowsett would be involved with much of the development of Prittlewell, buying up land and building houses as the town expanded over the next three decades, helping him to make his fortune. In the council elections of 1875, Dowsett stood as a candidate seeking membership of the local board of health, his main election address was expressing concerns about the pier. Continuing his interest and service to the town he would in 1892 become Southend's very first Mayor and a Justice of The Peace. A great achievement for the son of a humble bookmaker.

High Street

In the late 1870s he applied to the council to build his own shop and house at 39 High Street, the building stretched back into Alexandra Street. Here he would not only run his hardware, china and glassware shop, but use the address for his business as an estate agent. Sadly in January 1878, when the last of his eight children were born (Herbert) his wife Eliza of twenty years, died in childbirth. Three years later he married Clarissa Bentall, a member of the well known farming family of Leigh-on-Sea. They would have three daughters. Further activity on the High Street would see him buying land on the corner of the High Street and what would become known as Queens Road and further alterations and additions to his shop at 39. 1905 Thomas Dowsett had a operation for an internal growth and seemed to make good progress but in 1906 he passed away. In his will he left £222,713. 13s 6d.

High Street

Hairdressers

A visit to the hairdressers dates back thousand of years, with hairstyles changing with the decades, from curls to the downright outrageous. In the early part of the 18th century many hairdressers were for men. Today the premises are more likely to be called a "salon" and offer eyebrow waxing, manicures and blow-dries. One thing that I doubt has ever changed is the opportunity to sit back relax and talk about life's happenings. Today hairdressers are few and far between on the High Street.

Samuel Zucker
1859-1922

Born in Austria around 1859 he emigrated to England arriving in London in the 1880s. Next stop was Bournemouth where he had a hairdressers before moving on to Prittlewell where the last of his six children was born in 1906. Opening a shop at 21 High Street with his wife Bertha they ran a successful business until 1914 when the sinking of the Lusitania caused rioting in the area and their shop was attacked. They received compensation from Southend Corporation.

John Currie

From Liverpool where he was born in 1851, he had taken a shop on the High Street by 1873 with his wife Mary who was his assistant. Their son (who later worked with them) was born here in 1874 followed by two daughters. The hairdressers was successful enough to employ James Dunning from Somerset as well as members of the family. The Curries stayed until the 1890s.

Miscellaneous

The twenties and thirties saw William Sharp at 160 (in the 1940s and 50s Scott and Scrotton occupied the same address). Doric Ladies Hairdressers at number 132c and Mrs Kelley had an establishment at number 25, with S Underhill at number 10 offering the ladies hair care into the 1950s.

SNIPPERS BEAUTY SALON

Any woman will be pleasantly surprised to receive a gift of Beauty Therapy, which can include sun-tanning, slimming treatments, facials and skin treatments, Depilex painless epilation, waxing, manicures and hairdressing.

Vouchers available from £3 to £100.

**84 High Street, Southend-on-Sea, Essex
Tel. Southend 610940**

Xe24

1970s

32

High Street

Photographers

We take photography for granted these days, even using our mobile phones to record events, yet just two generations ago the average family didn't even own a camera. When they were invented in the 1800s they would have been far too expensive, instead they would go to the nearest photographic studio to take family portraits. By the 1900s you could hire a photographer to record weddings or christening and for many families today, the only photographs passed down the family are these rather staged and often unsmiling snapshots of their family events. With the outbreak of the First World War many had portraits taken of their men folk in their uniforms. Photography remained expensive and only the well to do could afford a camera, so there was still room for the many photographic studios springing up in towns and cities. Around the 1930s and 1940s mass production meant family's began to buy their own cameras but they were still beyond the reach of many.

High Street Photographers
1880s

Solman Popelestopp and his father-in-law Emphraine Lawton as well as his daughter shared number 24 as a studio. But by 1883 they had returned to London where Lawton had been born, followed soon after by the death of Popelestopp who was a native of Demark. For Emphraine Lawton (who previously had been a furniture maker) photography continued to be his occupation right up to his death in 1901.

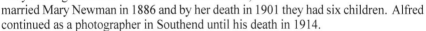

1890s

Alfred Laister Shepherd had a studio in what was known then as "Maypole House" calling his company "Day and Light Studios". Born in London in 1868, he married Mary Newman in 1886 and by her death in 1901 they had six children. Alfred continued as a photographer in Southend until his death in 1914.

1900s

William Tyler Evans was a photographer as early as 1901, when just 17, working and supporting his mother (a widow) who was paralyzed. His father, who had died before he was born, was also called William and had been the licensed Victualler of the Falcon Public House on Marine Parade. Marrying Christina White in July 1906, his mother was to die in December of that year. By 1911 his studio was at 19 the High Street and he now called himself a master photographer and was father to two daughters. William died here in 1962.

High Street

1922–1930

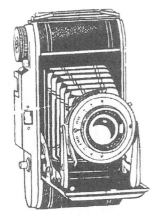

Boydes Studio Photographers and Caterers! From around 1922 until the 1930s, Boydes advertisements' were to offer to take family portraits or to cater for that special event. A strange combination, but true.

1937

Undoubtedly the most famous photographic shop on the High Street was Dixons, not named after its founders, but because the name (chosen at random) fitted above the door. Charles Kalms born in Russia and Michael Mindel, whose photographers (Mindel and Faraday) was at 340 Oxford Street, London, while Kalms was selling advertising space for the underground. They went into business opening Dixons Studios Limited, in the High Street at number 32, in 1937. With the outbreak of the Second World War, Dixons flourished because of the demand for portrait photography, from those going off to war (much like the demand in the First World War) so they opened a number of studios across London. By peacetime, demand had fallen and all but one of the studios in London and their business in Southend remained open. In 1948 Charles son Stanley (aged 16) joined the firm, a young man with vision he was to transform Dixons. The company began advertising new and second hand photographic products and laid the foundation for mail order. Dixons began to appear on high streets across the country and became a major retailer. Stanley Kalms went on to be Lord Kalms of Edgware. Charles Kalms and Michael Mindel both died in the 1970s.

1940s

Margaret Clarke first had a studio at 126 Broadway Leigh-on-Sea as early as 1927. Was she one of thousands of woman unable to marry because so many men had died in the First World War and had been forced to find an occupation? Throughout the 1930s/1940s Margaret had a studio on the Broadway Leigh, moving to Southend High Street by 1948, remaining at number 132c High Street until 1956 when a move to Clarence Street took place. Margaret Clarke continued to offer her photographic services until the 1960s, dying here in 1987.

With the growth of visitors, Southend had its share of photographers that walked among the trippers offering to record their visit to the seaside.

High Street

Owen Wallis
1851–1932

Many people remember Owen Wallis on the High Street, as a shop supplying many of their daily needs.

Owen Wallis,
Furnishing and General
Ironmonger, ...

47 HIGH STREET, SOUTHEND
(ESTABLISHED 1885)

Specialities :—

Table Cutlery,

Pocket Knives, Scissors,

Choice Designs in
Electro Plated Goods.

Trunks and Dress
Baskets.

Large Stock of Garden Tools and Lawn
Mowers.

Deliveries three times daily in Westcliff, Southchurch and Prittlewell.

Owen Wallis was born in Northamptonshire 1851 and was the son of a plumber. Aged only 20 he could be found working as a shop assistant in an ironmongers near his home, where he was employed for at least another 10 years. Marriage in 1885, was followed by a move to Southend and the opening of his own ironmongers. The birth of first son Owen quickly followed in 1886, with another son Harold, three years later in 1889. His first shop was at 41 High Street where it sold everything from lawn mowers, bicycles, perambulators, paint, polishes, brushes and brooms. Catastrophe struck in July 1900 and the following report was in the local paper.

The centre of Southend from the High Street to Weston and Clarence Roads was hit by a massive fire which destroyed a number of buildings. The fire started in Wallis's Ironmongery stores, due to the volatile reaction of three benzoline barrels being directly affected by the sun. They eventually exploded engulfing the premises in flames. It did not help that the next door premises were of a similar trade and its contents too helped keep the fire burning and spreading. Weston Chambers in Weston Road, made up of a few public offices such as the clerk to the local magistrates and the Southend Unionist and Conservative Club were soon fully alight. Many valuable records were lost. A number of businesses were either completely destroyed or partly damaged due to the low water pressure afforded to the firemen.

It must have been a spectacular but frightening occurrences and the Wallis family might have been forgiven for leaving town after such a devastating fire, but they remained another ten years. 1911 census found the whole family and their ironmongers at 61 High Street, where previously it had been at 41. The business was sold along with the name in 1920s and remained in the town until well into the 1980s.

© R Dilley

William Henry Luker
Lukers Brewery

Lukers Brewery once stood in Whitegate Road (later known as High Street) where many years later the site was converted into the Astoria Cinema, then became the Odeon. The Brewery had started life in Southchurch Road (formally called Brewery Road). They moved in 1869 to just off the High Street before the final move onto the main thoroughfare with a new and quite substantial building. As their business expanded they would go on to own The Hope and Middleton Hotels as well as the Blue Boar and White Horse in Southchurch. By owning these premises this ensured the public houses sold their beer. They also owned a brewery in Rayleigh.

The building was demolished in 1929

Far from the Luker family being generations of brewers their father William had been a carpenter and glassier with his sons plumbers, builders and carpenters. The Luker family came from Farringdon in Berkshire where they all lived until the early 1860s, when or why the change to brewing during this decade is not known. But in 1861 they were living on the same street as a Joesph Neate who was a Brewer. Were they influenced to change profession on seeing his work had a greater return, an unanswered question I'm afraid. There were originally four brothers John 1826, William 1828, Robert 1832 and Henry 1834. William was the only brother not to be a partner in the business. Leaving his three siblings to build their brewery empire here in Southend and Rayleigh. A partner outside of the family circle was acquired in 1888 a John George Baxter from Wanstead, Essex, who was a wealthy fish merchant, most probably injected the money needed to develop the Brewery. Henry Lucker was also trading in the town as a wine and spirit merchant in 1881. Married in 1873, to Ellen Lucking, whose father Christopher was a well known corn merchant here in the town, they were to have four children and it was to be the eldest son Allan, who would by the 1900s be a director of the business. Moving away and taking up residence in Kensington at the end of 1890, Henry, wife and son Stanley who was an undergraduate at Cambridge were to remain

---

Henry Luker & Co., Ltd.
THE BREWERY
Southend - on - Sea

Like a **LUKER** ?
TRY ONE

Ask for one at their Local Hotels as follows :

SOUTHEND - ON - SEA—Middleton Hotel, Hope Hotel, Castle Hotel, Britannia, Sutton Arms, Park Hotel.

PRITTLEWELL—Blue Boar Hotel, Railway Hotel.

SOUTHCHURCH—White Horse Hotel, Rose Inn.

LEIGH-ON-SEA—Carlton Hotel, Smack Inn, Peter Boat.

EASTWOOD—Woodcutters' Arms.

Sparkling Ale *in Crates, containing Four*
Single Stout *Quarts*
obtainable at all the above Houses

---

here until 1903 when Henry, on holiday in Surrey, passed away at a local hotel. His son was to continue at the brewery until the end of the 1920s, leaving the site derelict until 1934 when the Astoria Cinema was built on the site.

Robert moved to Hampshire with his family, becoming a Brewer and Spirit merchant there until his death in 1897, leaving over £10,236, a considerable sum for the time. Stanley fought in the First World War, as a member of the Royal Engineers, Allan Luker died in Sussex in 1931.

1879

The employers of Luker and Co enjoyed their annual excursion on Saturday, in fine weather. Leaving Southend on the 8am train, the party were some forty strong including members of the Luker family. Their destination, Regents Park and the Zoological Gardens.

1917

The brewery owned by Lukers at Rayleigh was forced to close after 122 years, due to the restrictions placed on the licensing trade as the result of the First World War. The Brewery had originally been built by a Mr Cross in 1795.

1923

The internment of William Henry Horner, who had been a carman at the brewery for over twelve years took place on the 8th September 1923. The coffin was conveyed from his home to the church on the brewers dray he had driven during his employment. William Horner was a local man born at Eastwood in 1855.

1934

In 1934 William Nancarrow died in his seventy fourth year. He had been a long standing employee of the company until its closure in the 1920s. He joined the firm in 1855 as a confidential clerk, rose to be the accountant, completing his employment as the manager. William had moved here with his new wife Amy Taylor and their five children would all be born in the family home in Princes Street. His daughters Isabel

and Margery never married and remained in the district until passing away 1954 and 1966. Edith married Stanley George Last in 1909. His son Ronald became an accountant but died just three years after his father his brother Caleb was a pawnbroker. William's wife Amy died in 1918. Today (2016) where once stood the brewery there are an assortment of shops.

Robert Arthur Jones
1849–1925

ONE OF THE SIGHTS
OF SOUTHEND
IS THIS SPLENDID SHOP.

FINEST STOCK OF DIAMOND RINGS, BROOCHES and
BRACELETS in the Eastern Counties.

Mr. R. A. Jones is an acknowledged expert in Diamonds.

76 & 78 HIGH STREET.
Founded 1890. *Telephone 1214.*

OVER 100,000 PRESENTS from 1/- to £1,000.
x'u

R A Jones came to the High Street and opened what was to became a successful jewellers with an ornate and very distinctive clock above the shop–still in evidence today. He went on to became one of the towns great benefactors.

You may not have purchased from his jewellers but you couldn't fail to notice the shop when walking by. Robert Arthur Jones was born in 1849 in West Derby, Lancashire the son of a watchmaker, John Jones from Wales. By 1871 Arthur was boarding in Liverpool with an uncle and his family, employed locally as a clock/watchmaker. Moving on to Staffordshire he met Emma Pedley daughter of an engraver, whom he married in 1878, together they had two sons, Edward Cecil 1883 and Arthur 1885. The move to Southend came in 1890 when for the first time R A Jones was self employed, how he financed this venture is unclear. His jewellers might have been a great success, but in 1912 his wife passed away, this led to the first of many generous gifts to the people of Southend-on-Sea. In 1913 he presented to the school children of the town Jones Memorial Ground with ornate gates in memory of his wife. The gift had cost him £9,000.

R A Jones in 1913

R. A. JONES & SONS,
The County Jewellers.

JONES'S CLOCK, SOUTHEND, THAMESMOUTH.
Established 1890.   CONTRACTORS TO THE CORPORATION.   Telephone 37y.

Marketing was key to his success and the use of adverts in the local paper and especially during the First World War.

Southend's Treasure House
A WONDERFUL SELECTION OF BEAUTIFUL GIFTS
The County Jewellers, 76 & 78 High Street
FOUNDED 1880   Telephone: MARINE 1901

1935

Southend and Westcliff Graphic
1916
R A Jones for rings. We give and always have given since 1890 a genuine present with every £100 spent

Do not hoard your old jewellery but sell it to help the local war funds, We are pleased to offer exceptionally high prices for diamonds and precious stones, old jewellery gold watches, silver plate and old artificial teeth (yes teeth).

On the 17th of January 1913 R A Jones and Sons reserved two rows of seats for his staff at the Empire Theatre for a performance of Cinderella. They were also each given a box of chocolates to enjoy during the performance.

R A Jones was elected as Vice President of The Railway Association in the 1900s.

The wonderful memorial to his wife in Sutton Road Cemetery

Priory Park was formally opened by the Duke of York on the 14th July 1920

In memory of his wife he donated Victory Sports Ground to the town.

Interior of R A Jones

Soldiers in a Literary Competition

Prizes given by Mr R A Jones for the best descriptive article on the Christmas festivities at Queen Mary's Hospital were presented on Tuesday in an interval of a concert at the hospital. The prizes were a silver cigarette case, and three silver Vesta cases. The judges were Miss Sant, Miss Barlow and Mr Jones. Mr Jones recently gave three silver rose bowls for the best decorated wards at Christmas. The cigarette case bore the inscription "Literally competition between the hospital patients for the best descriptive article in prose or verse Christmas 1915 at Queen Mary's Hospital" won by Bombardier R J Rinder, the winner of the second prize was Sapper A G Rich RND Engineers, Russia Ward and the third prize went to Corporal G H Gladman, Albert Ward. In the last case the writing was done by the left hand, the writer having lost his right arm. There were twenty two competitors.

1918

The Military Cross to Lieutenant Edward Cecil Jones for conspicuous gallantry while acting as a forward observation officer. His post was shelled incessantly throughout the day, but he succeeded in maintaining communication during the battle and directed the shooting of his battery with marked success. The information he obtained was of the utmost value.

Like his father Edward was involved with the town. 1933 saw him as the Honourable Secretary of the Southend-on-Sea District Voluntary Hospital Carnival Association, (the carnival is still going strong today) and of course the school Cecil Jones is named after him. Edward Cecil Jones died in 1967, the store continued trading until 1970 but then had a change of use. First a news agents then Dixons (electrical) and currently 2016 it is the "Yours" ladies wear shop.

Bequests

Undoubtedly the most well know gift from Arthur Jones to the town was what would become known as Priory Park. Having purchased the old Prittlewell Priory in a state of disrepair with three hundred acres of surrounding land from the Scratton family in 1917. R.A. Jones then bequeathed it to Southend Corporation for public use. Later he donated a memorial stone that stands outside the Priory and a large drinking fountain, still in evidence today. Subsequently the corporation restored the Priory and the land at a cost of £7,300 the building was then opened free of charge to everyone, on May 15th 1922 (delay due to the war). The gates to Priory Park have plaques to commemorate their benefactor.

The curator of the Priory was one William Pollitt from Lancashire, where he was born in 1888. William was also the towns public librarian, a position he would hold for many years. He died in Southend 1963, leaving his worldly goods to his wife Ada.

1921 saw the last of R A Jones gifts to the town, when the area known as Victory Sports Ground was opened in memory of the sportsmen who had died in the First World War. The ground was managed by Southend Council as it is today and is where many cricket matches still take place. Robert Arthur Jones died in 1925 leaving the jewellers and the sum of £45,297. His son Edward Cecil continued with the business which was severely damaged during the Second World War.

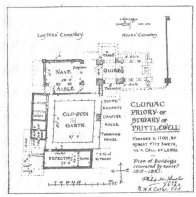

Council Plan of Priory 1922

Liptons

Lipton's was founded by Thomas Johnson Lipton in Scotland where he opened his first small provision store. Successful, he expanded first in Scotland then opened stores all over the country. His most famous product was Lipton's Tea, still available today. Liptons was originally at 74 High Street before moving to number 80.

Once again I have been supplied with photographs and information from Ernest Wells, who with his father (also Ernest) used to work at the Southend branch of Liptons. His father joined the store in the 1930s but with the outbreak of war he joined up, serving in the army. When hostilities ceased he returned to his old position at Liptons where rationing was to last into the 1950s and counting the points at the end of every day paramount. Lipton's like most stores in 1950/60s were still offering the customer personal service, but this would come to an end with the introduction of supermarkets. Although Liptons did become self service the day of the more personal approach to shopping was coming to an end. One area that the shop was forward thinking was the introduction

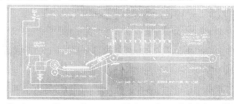

High Street

● METHOD OF OPERATION

The method of operation visualised is based on the principle of providing for the customer a printed list of all the goods carried by the machine. A sample list is shown on Page 16. The price of each article sold appears on the ticket and each article is given a stock number.

The salesman fills in the ticket in accordance with the customer's requirements and hands it to the cashier. The cashier presses out the numbers of the stock items on a row of ten push-buttons marked 0, 1, 2, 3, 4, 5, 6, 7, 8, 9. If the stock number is 78, she pushes the push-button 7 followed by the push-button 8. As soon as she has thus keyed up all the items required, the total cost of these items appears on a set of indicator lamps. She reads this off and writes it on the ticket, which she hands to the customer as she collects the money. The ticket received by the customer thus contains a complete description of the goods that he ordered, the price of each and the total cost, which later he can check up with the utmost ease. No printing devices are necessary, since all the printing is already on the tickets when they come from the printers.

While the cashier has been collecting the money, the goods have arrived at the packing counter. The last article reaches the counter within 7 seconds from the time the last push button is depressed. The cashier may then proceed to deal with another customer.

For large installations, many extra facilities can be provided in order to speed up the delivery still more.

▶ PRICING FACILITIES

The photograph on this page shows the pricing frame whereby the prices of the different articles are fixed. The first wire on this frame represents a halfpenny, the next eleven wires represent 1 to 11 pence, and the remaining wires represent 1 to 10 shillings. If an item cost 3/11½, then three wires are connected by soldering onto the pricing frame wires marked 1/-, 11d. and ½d. If the price changes later to 1/10½ the wire which was on the 11d. lead is changed to the 10d. lead. Thus the work of changing the price of an article consists of a moment's soldering. A power outlet is provided on the machine for a soldering iron for this purpose. All such changes are carried out by the supplier under the service and maintenance agreement, but no objection is raised to the shopkeeper making the change should he desire to do so.

This photograph was taken to the side of Liptons (Tylers Avenue). Mr Carver the manager (white hair) is standing in the middle of the back row. Ernest Wells Snr front right.

Staff members names unknown   *Ernest Wells Snr with pipe*

All photographs courtesy of Ernest Wells Jnr.

Today the cellars of Liptons, in Tylers Avenue are occupied by The Pipe Of Port.

High Street

Tomassi's

Tomassi's has been catering for visitors and locals of Southend-on-Sea since the 1930s. I can well remember my mother and aunt taking me to the old Tomassi's in the 1950s and ordering themselves knickerbocker glorys. To my young eyes they looked enormous and I looked on in amazement and wonder that anyone could devour anything of such large proportions. Today I have no such problem.

TOMASSI'S ORIGINAL
The Downstairs Cellar
BOUZY ROUGE

ESTABLISHED 1931

We've been serving SOUTHEND FAMILIES for over 50 years. We started with an Ice Cream/Coffee Shop and now we have three restaurants, all licensed — The Original, The Bouzy Rouge & the Downstairs Cellar — all serving delicious food and scrumptious ice cream.

We are open every day and do a SPECIAL SUNDAY LUNCH EACH SUNDAY

You can't miss us — coming up Pier Hill, we're the first Restaurant on the right in Southend High Street, and thanks to all of you, we're still growing and going.

Telephone Southend (0702) 67368 for further details or call at 16a-20, High Street, Southend-on-Sea

Tomassi's -
where
good food
costs less.

Pasquale Tomassi
1884–1957

Moving from Italy to Langley Park Durham, Pasquale Tomassi founded the family firm in 1912, using his wife Marianna's dowry. Money well invested, they lived and built up the business while living on Front Street, Durham until about 1932. When first coming to Southend-on-Sea they had a shop in the arches under the pier but had by the 1940s opened the downstairs cellar restaurant "Bouzy Rouge" at number 20 High Street. Tomassi's were among the first in Essex to introduce the Gaggia coffee machine (made in Italy) and to invest in a triple hedda ice cream machine. Pasquale Tomassi died in 1957 leaving his son, known as Tony to continue the family business.

Anthony Tomassi
1925–2012

His early years were spent in County Durham, until Tony Tomassi moved with his parents to Southend-on-Sea around 1932. When war broke out he returned to Durham and became a "Bevin Boy" working at a coalmine. For this he received many years later, the Bevin badge of recognition, although he was among the lucky ones and worked on the tramways above ground.

> Bevin Boys were largely conscripted young men and volunteers
> who worked in the coalmines during the Second World War.
> This vital role supplied coal for the war effort.

In 1951 Tony married June English, their three children are Anna, who was one time leader of Southend Council, her daughter Antonia following family tradition by renovating the old shelter on the seafront in 2015 and opening the Oyster Creek serving among other items gelato ice cream.

High Street

The restaurant at number 20 continued to thrive over the next 40 years, a popular destination for trippers and those living locally. In the 1980s they were forced to re-locate when the area was demolished and replaced with the giant shopping complex known as The Royals. Today they can be found at number 9 High Street, still serving meals at reasonable prices and offering their legendry ice-creams including the old fashioned knickerbocker glory.

Pasquale Tomassi's original restaurant in the High Street, where the family remained until the development of the area in what is now known as The Royals.

TOMASSI

Downstairs

LUNCHTIMES
Monday to Sunday
12-2.30 pm.

LICENSED RESTAURANT

EVENINGS
Wednesday to Saturday

AWARDED THE BRITISH STEEL CORPORATION - EGON RONAY
STAINLESS STEEL CLEAN KITCHEN AWARD

20 High Street, Southend.   Telephone (0702) 67368

The Tomassi family still own the restaurant today. Offering their famous deserts (2016)

46

High Street

Garons

By 1947 Garon's owned thirty seven shops, ten restaurants, cafes and a cinema, later adding a large banqueting suite at Victoria Circus to their portfolio but it was through Henry Fuller Garon (b 1833) and his wife Margaret that the Garon dynasty originated.

Henry's parents were John and Elizabeth Garon, the family were first noted in Prittlewell in 1839, advertising John as a painter. Their large family of three daughters and six sons are to be found on the 1841 census. When his father died in 1848, Henry moved out of the family home into a boarding house at no 5 High Street where his occupation was the same as his late father. Within ten years he had opened a grocers shop on East Street and married Margaret Bertha Shead who came from London. Her father Thomas was an egg dealer, perhaps this is how they met when Henry was looking for provisions for his shop. As their family grew (six children) they moved to North Street and opened another grocery store and it was here Henry died in 1877, leaving Margaret and the family to carry on the business into the 1880s, with a young Harry (b1863) as one of her assistants. It was to be this son who perpetuated the name of Garon's, opening their first shop at 64 High Street in 1885. By the 1890s he was living on Tylers Avenue with his family and listed as a butcher and provisions merchant. His brother Frederick was a butchers assistant, with sister Annie his clerk. They also opened a bakery, fish shop and ironmongers as well as the cinema and food outlets. By the 1900s the family were very evident on the High Street and beyond – having bakers and tea rooms in Leigh-on-Sea. Their first banqueting suite was at number 94 High Street and in 1921 they applied for an Ale Licence. Harry's three sons were to be part of the Garon's empire, Frank was in charge of the bakery, Percy restaurant manager, Harry, director.

Harry and Margaret Garon's Children

Emma 1861–1916   Married Richard Steward Undertaker in 1887. Richard died in 1945 and their only son Victor carried on the family's well known funeral parlour.

Henry 1865   He married Edith Annette Harvey

Frederick 1864–1901   Was employed in the family business but later was the publican of the Blue Boar.

Frederick Garon

Annie 1866–1946   Married Charles Bayliss

Kate 1868–1921   Married George Warren. His father had a boot makers at 13 High Street from the 1880s. On his death George took over the business.

Annie Garon

Photographs Permission of C Bayliss

Frank 1870   Died when nine years old

The family were also well known as estate agents in the 1800s, before opening many of their food stores.

The advertisements below were advertising their wares in the 1900s.

Locations 1920

66	The People's Restaurant
66A	Fish Shop
95	Silver Grill and Tea Rooms
94A	Bakery
96	Butchers
98	Fish and Poultry
98A	Table Delicacies and Provisions

High Street

Fire

On the 29th January 1897 a fire was spotted at one of their restaurants at 11.30 at night. A postman discovered the blaze on the High Street. An investigation revealed that an overheating refrigerator had ignited the matchboard ceiling. The fire brigade were duly called and put out the blaze before further damage was done.

Henry Garon was in 1902 to hold the rank of Captain in the volunteer fire brigade. Founded in 1877 by The Southend Local Board the fire station was first sited at Market Place moving in 1901 to Tylers Avenue. After 1914 when the County Borough was inaugurated the brigade was administered by the Fire Brigade sub-committee.

Operation

The local paper reported in 1909, that Councillor Garon was progressing satisfactorily after his operation on June 4th of that year.

Funeral

The funeral took place on Friday 11th November 1911 of Harry Garon. Spectators lined the route from the deceased's residence in Warrior Square to St Mary's Church Prittlewell. All the shops in the Broadway closed and a large number of tradesmen attended. The cortege was headed by a mounted constable, behind which followed contingents from the Southend Leigh and Shoebury fire brigades. Following were two open carriages filled with floral tributes. There were eight carriages containing relatives and friends. Also attending were the Mayor, councillors and over 200 employees of H Garon and Co.

Harry Garon had died following a serious operation for the removal of an abscess on the brain. He was only 49 years old he left a widow three sons and three daughters.

Summons

In 1914 Garons was prosecuted for selling meat under a false trade description.

Conditional Exemption

On the 26th January 1917 Harry Garon general manager of Garons Ltd applied for conditional exemptions. He stated that he had had no holidays since the war broke out and had a minimum working day of fourteen hours. He stated that a hundred and forty of his employees were now in the army or had been killed. The situations of those who might return were being kept open. The company made applications for a number of men in their employ who should be given conditional exemptions.

Arthur David Cotgrove
1863 – 1953

Cotgrove is a surname synonymous with old Leigh and fishing and Arthur David Cotgrove was no exception coming from at least two generations of fisherman including his father David. In later life David Cotgrove 1830–1909 would be a fishmonger, selling rather than catching fish, living in Prittlewell as opposed to the Old Town, Leigh.

David Arthur Cotgrove, born in Leigh 1865, did not entirely follow family tradition and go to sea. In the 1880s he was a carpenters apprentice and lived with the family on Park Street, Prittlewell. In 1895 he married Martha Ratcliffe Bewer and that same year submitted plans to Southend Corporation to build a house and shop on the high street on what became number 18. Plans were agreed and the property was soon built and occupied. Arthur made another submission in 1897 for alterations to his shop. 1913 draft tenancy for 11 and number 16 High Street were drawn up. Number 11 called The White House. The other, part of the tenancy, number 16 went to David Cotgrove–fishmonger. During his time on the High Street Cotgrove would be listed over the years as a restaurateur coffee house keeper and dairyman. Most of us remember Cotgroves as just a restaurant serving the trippers and locals. Arthur and his wife Martha had six children, three girls three boys, of whom two Frank Reginald and Edward Victor were involved with the business, Edward was a company director, Frank a caterer. Frank was married twice his first wife was Jessie Rowland and they had four children, she died in 1955. Two years later he married Florence Cooper, but his demise in 1964 meant the marriage lasted only nine years. When Cotgroves closed in the 1970s Tomassi's took over the building.

Staff 1953

Frank Reginald Cotgrove

© Photographs by kind permission
N Cunningham

The London Hotel

Known variously as the London Tavern or Hotel, my memories of the establishment in the 1960s was as The London. A pub fronting the High Street and a dance hall at the back, with the entrance in Tylers Avenue. I used to attend the regular Thursday dance with friends and later my future husband.

The London Hotel
© *Antony Pelling*

Edward Parsons
1833- 1899

Moving to Prittlewell around 1854, Edward Parsons was a Potter, having served an apprenticeship in Lambeth where he was born in 1833. Marrying a local girl Ann Elizabeth Thipthorpe in 1856 they were to be found on North Street, Prittlewell where their sons Albert 1859 and William 1860 were born. Why the change of direction from potter to licensed victualler where Edward had no experience is a mystery.

A mishap on Foulness saw Edward Parsons miss his footing when getting out of his pony and trap, severely injuring his leg. A Mr Popplewell passing in his trap took him back to Southend where Dr. Deeping attended to his quite bad fracture. The report added that fortunately he had an accident insurance policy.

From 1870 until his death in 1879 Edward and Ann were the landlords of The London Hotel. In 1879 their son Albert was to die, just a few months later Edward was to pass away leaving just William who died in 1895. Ann having remarried to a William Tyler who had been the head waiter at The Royal Hotel, he died in 1894 leaving Ann a widow for the second time.

Henry Brown
Resident at the hotel between 1894- 1898

Arthur Wilson
Again another short stay. Arthur Wilson was landlord between 1898–1901

High Street

William Hines
1854 - 1923

The son of a Licensed Victualler it will come as no surprise to find William Hines born 1854 in London following the same occupation. In 1871 he was working as a manager of a public house in St Clements London, where he met his future wife Annie Maria James. Annie was working as the housekeeper. They married the following year and by the 1880s William was the Licensed Victualler of The Duke of Clarence, in the Mile End Road. Moving on in the 1890s he was at a public house in Camberwell. What would be their last move, they came to The London Hotel in 1901, with four of their children of whom one Lillian married a Frederick William Pelling whose father owned a large provisions store in Grays ,Essex.

William Hines
© *Antony Pelling*

September 1915 William Hine was summoned under The Defence of the Realm Act for opening his premises to members of His Majesty's Forces out of hours. A policeman passing at 11pm saw soldiers leaving the public house with tankards of beer. The mayor said the bench regarded this as a very serious matter. In his defence Hine had claimed it was a employee who had committed the offence but the bench said he was responsible for staffs actions and fined him £10. A large sum of money in those days.

During 1918 William and Annie, like so many during that time, were to lose a son to the First World War. Ernest born in London in 1887, had been serving in France with the Royal Horse Artillery. He left his effects of £118.15s to his father who was now retired.

Although William Arthur Hine passed away in Marylebone in 1923, he was still a resident of Southend and so was buried here, as was his wife who joined him six years later. From the 1920s onwards The London was first owned by Home Counties Trust Ltd or The Trust Houses Ltd. The day of the individual rather than the corporation was now becoming the norm.

As with other public houses The London had its share of meetings and mishaps.

1875

Liquidation proceedings. William Perkins innkeeper of The Blue Boar had a meeting with creditors at the London Hotel.

High Street

May 1881

A tradesmans supper was held with Mr F Garon in the Chair with Mr F Belcham Vice Chair. Other well known names present were, Wakerling, Boosey, Warren and Ingram.

Building Plans

General alterations and additions – 1891
Stable and coach house   – 1893
Porch to entrance hall – 1906

1892

Charles Story was charged with refusing to leave the hotel on June 30th. Mr Brown landlord, asked that the case be dismissed as Mr Story had apologised, but the bench still fined him 2s 6d and directed costs to be given to Mr Brown.

1901

Mr Edward Jeffery Howard died suddenly at The London Hotel. The deceased a retired publican was on a visit to his niece. He was 49 years of age.

1st December 1933

A fire at the hotel while the Southend Wheelers were enjoying dinner did not stop proceedings, even though water poured through the ceiling they continued with their meal! The fire destroyed three staff bedrooms at the top of the hotel and a waitress lost savings of £30 which were burnt. Considerable damage to the building was done by the water used to extinguish the flames. Three fire engines and an escape ladder attended and they found it necessary to cut a hole in the ceiling to get the hose into the roof. One guest bedroom was destroyed by the fire but the other two bedrooms were affected by the water.

1941

The hotel suffered a direct hit causing considerable damage.

2016

Today the site is occupied by a well known card company and for many people passing by unaware of its past history.

The site of The London Hotel today.
© B Edwards

Marlborough Hotel

MARLBOROUGH HOTEL RESTAURANT
FAMILY AND COMMERCIAL,

16 High Street, Southend.
(Close to Pier and Station).

Home Comforts combined with Luxury. Private Dining, Smoking and Coffee Room for Guests.

Spacious Dining Hall (Seating Accommodation for 300)
FOR PARTIES AND BEANFEASTS.

Terms Moderate. Bed and Breakfast from 4/6.
Entirely Redecorated. Under New Management.

SAM ISAACS, Ltd., Proprietors. Telephone 154.

The hotel, built at the bottom end of the High Street in the late 1890s only lasted until the 1920s. Although lavish accommodation was offered with a ballroom, which could be turned into a dining experience for four hundred people it did last the test of time. In a prime position for visitors it is hard to see why its presence in the town was so short.

George Henry Tipper

Born in London in 1838, he was known as a refreshment housekeeper from the 1880s. Marrying in 1883 he was soon a widower, moving to Prittlewell a year later. According to the Essex Records Office one George Henry Tipper applied to Southend Borough Council in 1897 plans to build a hotel and restaurant known as "Tippers" near the bottom end of the High Street. Two years before he had applied for a counterpart licence to serve food and drink in the pier refreshment rooms. His hotel was opened for business by 1899 and boasted a large luxury ballroom, lounge and forty bedrooms. And of course his well appointed restaurant. In a few short years he made quite a success of his various interests in the town including a coffee house in Alexander Road. Dying in 1903, address given as the High Street, probate was granted to John Friday Vickers, a Temperance Society agent and Thomas Dowset to distribute his legacy of £3312.

Thomas Dowsett

For a time Thomas Dowsett appeared to be the owner/manger of the hotel but there is little evidence of his time there. The period only ranged from 1903 until his death in 1906.

George Tipper also had a bakery in Alexander Street

Joseph Henry Harding

Between 1912–1914, Joseph Harding was listed at the premises, again either manger or owner.

Tipper Restaurant to the right of the photograph.

Permission of Southend Standard

Samuel Isaacs Ltd

From 1917–1925 the Sam Isaacs Company were the owners.

Alexandra House
27 High Street

Alexandra House was a drinking establishment selling among other things Porter *"a dark style beer developed in London from well hopped beers brown malt."* The earliest reference to the building seems to be around 1800. Not to be confused with the Alexandra Hotel. The public house stood on the corner of the High Street and Alexandra Street.

George Wakeling

George and Emma Wakeling nee Ingram were both native to the area. Marrying in 1862 they had two children, Emma who died here in 1972 and Thomas who was a medical student. Living with them was Emma's brother William a mineral water merchant. When George passed away in 1891 his wife continued to manage the pub until 1895, when she retired to Grove Road, Southend and was to live for many years supported by private means. Her income was such that she was able to employ two servants. Emma Wakeling died in 1922

William George Harvey

With his father Robert Harvey a publican at the Park Hotel, Park Street, Prittlewell, it was no surprise that his son George William Harvey followed suit. In the 1800s he worked as one of his father's barman before taking over the management of the Alexandra House from Emma Wakeling. He had worked for the Wakelings as a barman where he met an Ellen Harcup who became his wife in 1893, they went on to have two children, George Lionel and Minnie. William and Ellen managed the public house for many years until Ellen's death in 1924, a year later her husband left Alexandra House passing away in 1937.

In the 1900s a Henry Franks was landlord.

Modern Inns and Taverns Ltd

Owners from the 1920s onwards became a company or brewery, rather than an individual family. The Alexandra was still in business in 1948, but the final closure of the public house is unknown.

The building today 2016
© *Barry Edwards*

Middleton Hotel

The Middleton Hotel and public house was built and owned by Lukers Brewery. It was one of many the brewery built or owned to ensure the sale of their beer. Fronting the High Street the building stretched back to face the central railway station. Between 1899 and 1929, alterations were made by the owners. First in 1897, a new office in 1899, a loft over the stables in 1911 with further alterations to the building in 1912 then as late as 1928/9. The hotel was party to a billiards exhibition in 1870 when a match was arranged which was attended by over a thousand people as well as the local gentry. 1893 a Freemasonry festival of the Priory Lodge was held at the hotel when Brother Alfred Vandervood was installed for the coming year. The installation was followed by a banquet.

Hotel Keepers

Built 1860 the first Licensed Victualler was a widow, Elizabeth Cantor, who with her husband James had previously had a pub in Bromley. With her children, Ferdinand, who died here in 1926, son James who returned to London and passed away in 1919 and daughter Anne, they also employed a cook, barmaid and groom to help with the daily chores. Elizabeth died in 1876 leaving a £1000 in her will. Following her death a Bruce McNaly Johnson was landlord for eight years, before passing the hotel on to a Arthur George Renninson for just four years, Arthur moved on to run the Greyhound Public House in Tunbridge Wells where he died in 1916. James and Amelia Pritchard took over next and with their large family stayed at the Middleton for around ten years. William Thomas Buxton and his wife Emma were the next landlords from around 1898 until Williams death in 1900. A newspaper report that year stated

The funeral took place of Mr W T Buxton who for the past four years has been the proprietor of the Middleton Hotel. He was a known Freemason for over fifty five years but five months ago became seriously ill. The wake was held in the Masonic Lodge room at the hotel. He leaves a widow and three daughters. His wife continued running the hotel until 1910 when William Sherratt became the Licence Victualler.

—THE—

MIDDLETON HOTEL,

Family & Commercial,

—— **SOUTHEND-ON-SEA.** ——

Proprietor - - - - - WM. E. SHERRATT.

This Hotel is most centrally situated in the High Street, quite close to all places of amusement, Railway Stations and the Sea Front.

Recently Re-decorated and Electrically Lighted. Moderate Tariff. Real Comfort.

William Ellerton Sherratt had previously been a commercial traveller but in 1910 came to Southend with his wife Ada and took on the Middleton Hotel. With a staff of twelve including a Nicholas De La Gardelle from Luxembourg who worked as a barman. Surprisingly considering the number of staff not one was a local resident. The couple remained at the hotel until the late 1920s. William died in 1947 leaving over £7000.

The next tenant was John Charles Moss, who although born in London had been involved with local hotels for a number of years. First as landlord of the Grand Hotel Leigh-on-Sea, with his wife Flora. Their two sons Wilfred and Donald, were born there in 1901 and 1903. By 1909 they were managing the Pier Hostel, Grove Road, Southend. They moved into the Middleton in 1925 staying some twenty three years until John Moss died whilst still managing the hotel in 1948. Flora died here in 1955, their sons married and moved away.

BILLIARDS ! ! !

A GRAND MATCH WILL BE PLAYED

AT THE

MIDDLETON HOTEL, SOUTHEND,

On TUESDAY, MAY 3rd,

BETWEEN Mr. J. ROBERTS (Ex-Champion) and Mr. H. EVANS, the latter receiving 250 points in 1,000.

An early application for tickets is requested, as but a limited number will be issued. Play to commence at Eight o'clock. Tickets of admission 5s. each.

High Street

In 1950/60s an Olga Louse Henning was the proprietor and it was during the 1960s that I would visit the venue. Eventually retiring she was living in St Vincent's Road Westcliff when she died in 1978 leaving a healthy sum of money £66,920.

The High Street 1950s. The Middleton Hotel is on the left of the photograph.

Many years later Middleton Public House and Hotel would be split up into separate units. The section fronting on the High Street was for a time a pizza restaurant. In 1980 Derek and Rodney Oldham brought the Middleton pub after it had stood empty for some two years and renamed it The Dickens. With a Carvery and live music it proved a great success until they sold it six years later.

High Street

Hotel Victoria

The Hotel Victoria was a large rather splendid hotel opened in 1898, with electric light and steam radiators. At the top of the High Street visitors arriving by train could not fail to notice this rather splendid building. An item in a local newspaper reported This fine hotel was erected by Mr Philsopher J Burdett and was opened on Wednesday when it was visited by hundreds of local townsfolk. The town band under the direction of Mr A F Stevens entertained the crowd. Architects were Thompson and Greenhalgh. It was a shame after such a grand opening that in the evening John Burdett, son of the owner was injured in an accident. When moving timber from the back of the hotel, one of the horses bolted and in an attempt to stop it he was crushed against the wall. He broke his collar bone and sustained other injuries. On a much lighter note, in 1899 a rather ornate porch was added to the front of the hotel. A strange but seemingly terse notice was placed in the newspaper soon after opening, which stated "that any correspondence not addressed correctly ie Hotel Victoria would not be opened."

The Burdetts
Philsopher John Burdett was born in Leicestershire in 1839 the son of a tailor, he followed the profession until 1880 when he became the Licenced Victualler of the Grapes Tavern in London. He had previously married Elizabeth Amelia McCann in 1867 and their daughter Ruth was born soon after, but had died by 1875. Later they were to have two sons John George and William. John married Ethel Bates in 1898 a year before his father's grand hotel was built and the couple for a time were to be the manager and manageress when the Victoria opened. Sadly Philsopher's wife died in 1900 followed the year after with his own demise. The hotel had been quite successful during the Burdett's period and had employed up to fifteen servants. With the death of their father, William and John gave up the Victoria and by 1902 the premises was in the hands of a new owner.

High Street

Edwin Albert Broadhurst

Here in Southend from around 1902 until his death in 1910, Edwin Broadhurst had previously been a hotel manager in London along with his wife Fanny Shadbolt nee Shedden whom he had married in 1895. Uniquely for the period she had petitioned Charles Shadbolt for a divorce which was granted. Her son Ormonade's birth in 1886 would be registered as Ormonade Shedden, Shadbolt, but he would take the surname of his stepfather and in 1910 married in his adopted surname, the daughter of the next owner of the hotel. When Edwin died his wife was well provided for as in his will he left £4706 5s 6d this enabled her to move to the Channel Islands to live with her sister. During the Broadhurst's time at the hotel he offered Turkish baths, electric light throughout, motor garage and stabling, balls, banquets and dinners catered for.

1910

On January 4th a valet, employed at the Hotel Victoria, leapt from an upper window onto the crowed pavement below. Named as Samuel Adams he was taken to the local hospital but died later of his injuries.

Breach of Promise

Doris Cooper of Battersea claimed damages against Marcel Theus who had jilted her. The plaintiff was working in an umbrella shop in Southend in 1908 when she met the defendant, a Swiss, then employed as a chef at the Hotel Victoria. February 1909 he proposed they became engaged and arranged that a marriage take place on the 15th September. The plaintiff gave up her employment. Subsequently the defendant broke off the engagement. The jury assessed the damage at £35 with costs.

Criminal Act

George Earle a Potman, was remanded in custody having been found on enclosed premises for unlawful purposes at the Hotel Victoria he was sent for trial.

Clement Edward Morris

When he died the local paper reported "Mr Morris had been a licence victualler all his working life" this was in fact an inaccurate statement. From the 1880s to 1891 he had been variously a chair maker and a manufacturing upholsterer. Born in Suffolk in 1858, his first marriage to Annie produced five children. One of whom Maude will marry the stepson of the previous owner of the Victoria and ultimately run the hotel with her husband. Annie had died in the early 1890s and we find after marrying his second wife, Florence Hibberdine, in 1898 it was then he turned his attention to running a pub in London. Having moved to Prittlewell around 1910 they managed the Victoria together until Florence died in 1927, followed a year later by her husband. They had made the hotel one of the most successful in the area shown in the amount of money left in Clements will, £104,000 to be distributed thus:

His house in Dowset Avenue and personal effects to Ormonade and Maud Broadhurst, £5000 to daughter Dolly £4000 to his son Edward John. To Doctor Frederick Walker and Nancy Butcher £500 each. An annuity of £10,00 each to his sister-in-law Fanny Broadhurst and his sister Florina Cook. The residue of his estate in trust for his daughters Eva Jenkins, Maud Broadhurst and Daisy Black. There were also small bequests of £200 to Bertie Simmons (known as George the boots) and £100 to William Oddie, coachman.

The Hotel

During Clement Morris's time at the Victoria it had its share of events and happenings including this statement in the local press *"we understand that the partnership existing since May 1910 between Mrs Broadhurst and Mr C E Clement has been dissolved this week by mutual consent"*. The date 1916. As before the hotel will be under the personal supervision of Mr Morris who now becomes the sole proprietor.

1911 saw the Rochford Police Division entertained to dinner. Mr Wedd president (Edward Wedd was a Justice of the Peace, county councillor and landowner from Great Wakering) supported by the Mayor Alderman Ingram, members of the council and the Chief of Police.

1919 a dustman clearing out a bin in the yard of the hotel discovered the body of a newly born male baby. Appearances suggested the body had been there at least two days. On a lighter note a sale of property took place on Wednesday 10th May 1919, of 7-12 Rampart Street Shoebury, as there was no bid the auctioneers (Offin and Rumsey) said they would accept a very low bid. 1922 saw the Royal Arch Masons (Priory Chapter) hold a meeting at the hotel. The scribe was T Byford. That same year Priory Lodge Freemasons also had a meeting there. Talbot and White auctioneers conducted a sale in one of the conference rooms.

*Two photographs
showing the interior
of the hotel*

© P Wren

*The site today
© B Edwards*

High Street

Trams passing by the Hotel Victoria
By kind permission of Middleton Press

With Clement Edward Morris's death in 1928 his daughter Maude and husband Ormonade took on the management of the hotel. They had one child, Dora born in 1911. They remained as managers until 1937. Still living in the town, Ormanade died in 1947, his wife resided in Thorpe Hall Avenue with their daughter until her death in 1972.

IRA

In 1939 the greatest threat to the area came when there was a campaign of terror by the IRA on seaside resorts. Their target in Southend was the Hotel Victoria, a fire broke out simultaneously in several of the bedrooms. Each room had been booked by men using false names.

The hotel continued to dominate the top end of the High Street and I well remember it as a teenager, but change came in the 1970s when the area was redeveloped and a sale of a mixture of in-house goods took place:

Gold Lloyd Loom Chair – wicker table – carpets – green enamelled chest 3 3 feet long- upholstered sofa – blue and floral damask table clothes – sheets – pillowcases – towels – cutlery – 52 pint tankards – 3 beer pumps – royal typewriter –Kelvinator freezer.

How the sale went was not reported. For many years Barclays Bank occupied part of the site, but the large imposing building is no more.

John Rumbelow Brightwell

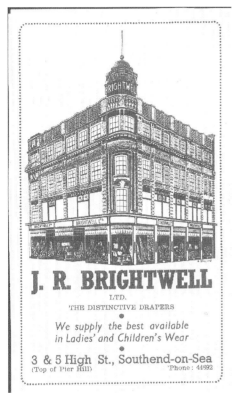

J. R. BRIGHTWELL
LTD.
THE DISTINCTIVE DRAPERS

We supply the best available
in Ladies' and Children's Wear

3 & 5 High St., Southend-on-Sea
(Top of Pier Hill)   'Phone : 44692

To most people hereabouts the name Brightwells is associated with his store at the far end of the High Street, close to the seafront, which closed in the 1970s. Like many businessmen coming into Southend in the Edwardian period, he saw an opportunity to make money by buying up land, becoming a developer, estate agent and money lender. This was at a time when the ancient parishes of Prittlewell and Southchurch saw their population rise from 27,299 in 1901 to 62,723 by 1911. But the gradual growth of the town prior to the 1900s had seen a need for extra housing. The Brightwell Estate Company was set up on the corner of London Road and Brightwell Avenue in 1908. I know this avenue well as I grew up there in the 1950s and 60s. Building plots were auctioned in the marquees set up by his company. Brightwell also owned property in Heygate Avenue and in 1912 he leased number 2 to William May, tailor and ladies costumier. 1919 he lent William Chignell, who had a hosier shop on the High Street, £1,450 to purchase a property also in Heygate Avenue. In 1925 he arranged a lease for five years on numbers 2 and 2a, for a Percy and Francis Bacon (brothers) on what was a double fronted dwelling and shop. He also owned number 19 High Street which in 1908 he had applied to the council for permission to carry out alterations.

Family History
Born in Mildenhall, Bury St Edmunds in 1849, the son of a tailor, the perfect background for a man who would go on to be a silk merchant and draper. In 1871 he was in Peterborough, working as a drapers assistant where he stayed until 1873 when he married Eliza Maria Pettitt. The couple moved directly to Prittlewell and opened their now well known establishment, moving into the living accommodation above the shop. It would not be until the late 1800s that

the family would move round the corner to a more prestigious address, number 15 Royal Terrace. The first of their five daughters Florence was born soon after they arrived here, she was joined by Helen, Kate, Ethel and Margaret. Another sister Evelyn was born in 1881, living only a short time and sadly the only boy born to

Ethel Brightwell and Samuel Underhill at their wedding at St John's Church, Southend

the couple, Frank, came in 1876, dying early in 1877. Of his five daughters, only two married. Katie to a Colin Campbell 1899. His occupation at the time was glove manufacturer, (an item sold by Brightwells) perhaps that is how they met when he sold his merchandise to her father. They moved to Islington where they had five children and Campbell changed his occupation to that of glass bottle merchant. The second daughter to marry was Ethel in 1913, when she became the wife of Samuel Underhill an insurance agent of Ealing in London. Florence and Helen (who never married) remained here in Prittlewell for a time after the death of their parents in the 1920s in 1933 they are shown as still resident at number 8 Royal Terrace later number 5. By the 1940s they had left the area. On their demise in 1961 and 1966 they were living together at the Savoy Hotel, Cheltenham. Their sister Margaret also a spinster, was living in the Rosemont Hotel, Tunbridge Wells when she died in 1967, leaving £15,850.

John Ruberlow Brightwell was a councillor, magistrate and Mayor of the town twice 1894 and 1895. He died a year after his wife Eliza in 1925 at the Royal Exeter Hotel Bournemouth.

Brightwells The Store
Coming to Southend and opening a small drapers in the 1870s was a shrewd move, as the town was beginning to grow and prosper. Picking what became the bottom end of the High Street, was a good place to choose, as in those days the Royal Hotel next door attracted the more salubrious visitors to the town and the Royal Library at the top of Pier Hill was well used by locals and holidaymakers. At first with his growing family they lived above the shop. Business was good and he was soon seeking the permission of the local council to make improvements. As early as 1878 he applied to build a workroom at the rear of his property. Over the years he replaced the windows and made several alterations and enlarged the floor space to take in the whole building. In 1909 under the Companies (Consolidation) Act of 1908 he formed the company of John Rumberlow Brightwell Ltd. This meant that there were now directors and shareholders. He listed the business as that of a silk merchant and milliner, outfitters, glover, hosier, dressmaker, dealer in household fittings and house furnisher and of course that of a draper.

1913

Brightwell's headed notepaper

Brightwells had up to eleven people working in the store at any given time as well as those who were employed in his workshop. In the 1880s he employed drapery assistants from Suffolk and Cambridge, with a Lousia Colien from Surrey as a milliner. In the 1890s closer to home, a Benjamin Moss was apprenticed to him for two years and Helen Kate Harvey was also to serve a two year apprenticeship. Helen would later became a dressmaker working from home. The family lived in Sutton Road and her father had been one of the new breed of auctioneers. In April 1913 John Brightwell staged a mannequin parade at the nearby Palace Hotel, also in that year he advertised for good bodice hands, wages 25/30s a week. In 1918 Brightwell spoke up for a member of his staff caught stealing. George Yewdall who had worked for the store for just over a year, as a buyer and manager, was caught stealing three skin rugs, value £4.14s,2d. He was of previously good character and his employer felt if convicted that it would result in the breaking up of his family. It was decided that if the bench allowed the prisoner to leave in the charge of a constable and go straight to the recruiting station and enlist in the army he would go free. This he duly did. Brightwells continued in name only until the 1970s.

Ravens

Ravens is still very much a part of Southend's shopping experience, in Cliftown Road (just off the High Street) they opened their first shop nearly 138 years ago. There cannot be many who have lived in the town for a long time who have not heard of the store, or shopped there. Speaking for myself when working locally in the 1980s and 90s I was sent out on more than one occasion to buy a leaving gift for a colleague, if a female member of staff I inevitably went to Ravens gift department, as they stocked such a wide variety of merchandise. Today you can expect the same friendly service that no doubt their ancestors provided all those years ago.

Family of Drapers

Behind the Ravens foundation were two people, Percy Raven (1875–1967) and his wife Gertrude Ellen Marshall (1878–1958). The couple married in Croydon, Surrey 1898. Percy's parents were William and Maria Anne Raven, in 1875, like his father Thomas, William had been a baker, later in life he was a sub–postmaster in Kent, sharing his premises with daughter Grace, selling confectionery. Gertrude was the daughter of a successful leather merchant in London, who travelled up each day from Surrey to the city. Their backgrounds being entrepreneurial, it is perhaps no surprise that by 1901 they had opened their own hosier and hatter shop on the Romford Road and in 1900 another at Southend-on-Sea. From the very beginning Gertrude worked alongside

Raven Children
© Raven Family

her husband in expanding the Ravens chain, except for the very early years when their children were born. Their son Cecil was just a year old in 1901, when brother Douglas joined the family. Siblings Irene 1905, Bernard 1907, was born in Southend with Ronald's arrival in 1917, when the family lived at Rayleigh. All of their sons were in time part of the business.

Percy Raven
CIVIL
AND
MILITARY
Tailor,
90 High Street,
Southend-on-Sea.
Telephone 154.
SPECIAL VALUE IN
Active Service Kit.   Officer's Field Kit.

The Ravens like so many families were caught up in the First World War. Tragically Frederick Raven one of Percy's brothers, who had been the manager of the juvenile outfitters, at 124 High Street in 1909, later died fighting in France in 1917.

Thankfully Percy's son Cecil, also fighting in France with the 3rd London Regiment, came home at the end of hostilities. Brother Ronald, who had managed the toy department of Ravens in the 1930s was not to be so

High Street

fortunate with the advent of the Second World War. Posted to the Far East, he was captured by the Japanese and ultimately died in a prisoner of war camp. Having kept a diary of his experiences, this was returned to the family by a fellow prisoner.

Attended by the Mayor, councillors, British Legion and other organisation as well as relatives of those killed in the war, the Ravens donated the memorial gates at Chalkwell Park we still pass them on our way to the car park. Irene Kellenberger–Ronald's sister formally opened them on the 30th April 1952.

For their four surviving children there would be marriage and a long life. Cecil (1899–1984) married Dorothy Cockerill, their son Roy and Thelma Stanton are the parents of the present owner Neil Raven. Douglas (1901–1992) married Margery Harwood. Irene 1905–1990 became Mrs Titus Kellenberger. Bernard (1907–1999) married Ruby Nicholls in Eastbourne where he had moved to open his own drapers business.

A Department Store or Two
Southend-on-Sea was by the 1890s fast becoming a very popular and ever growing sea side resort and place to live. Prosperity had come to the town when the

railway had finally reached the area in 1856. Percy and Gertrude Raven, having one shop in Romford, came to see the prospects on offer in the new fast growing High Street. Having liked what they saw they eventually opened for business at number 28 High Street–near York Road and almost opposite Woolworths in the late 1890s. Later they would have premises at 124 High Street but undoubtedly they are

Alterations at number 90 High Street

best remembered for their shop at number 90 High Street. In 1910 they submitted plans to Southend Corporation to make alterations to the building. The

biggest changes came when they had submitted plans in 1925, which after being approved saw scaffolding being erected in front of 90 and 92 High Street and

the major overhaul began in 1926. Large adverts were added to the scaffolding, to show the public they were still very much open for business. A local architect and the building company "Tibbles" were employed to turn a once ordinary shop into a multi–purpose store. In 1926 the impressive frontage was revealed with the main departments made ready for the Christmas trade of that year.

Ravens no. 90 High Street 1926

© Photographs the Raven Family

68

High Street

Ballroom and Restaurant

Early in 1927 the hairdressers was added, followed in the May by the 1st floor restaurant come ballroom. Having installed tables which could easily be removed, lunches would be served at the princely sum of one shilling and sixpence between the hours of noon and 3pm. As with diners today the best tables were by the windows, allowing you to see the passing crowds and of course be seen.

Items offered for sale in the 1920s were umbrellas, walking sticks and of course gloves. A hat and cap department for the gentlemen, shirts with separate collars Ladies ready to wear outfits, handbags and dressing cases and not forgetting the younger members of society, a juvenile department, selling the all important school uniforms.

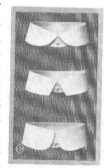

During the 1940s Ravens supplied officers uniforms and Christmas 1941 saw presents were posted to all evacuees around the country, but then rationing and other austere measures were introduced. Recovery for the clothing industry was slow following the end of the war and it was to be the 1950s before Ravens was fully operational again.

1930s saw the move to London Road (near Victoria Circus) as the family wanted to be seen as passengers came out of Victoria Station. To that end on Wednesday 10th July 1935 a staff party was held in the garden of Mr Raven's home in Rayleigh. Notably among them was Joan Capp (later Lowman) who was to become one of their longest serving members of staff, beginning her employment as cashier in the restaurant.

© Photographs the Raven Family

London Road Branch

Advertising their merchandise in the 1900s.

EXPERT IN BOYS' WEAR.

SCHOOL AND COLLEGE OUTFITTER

Telephone: 66x.

This Coat from 14/11.

WEST END STYLES at half the price you are accustomed to pay.

124, BROADWAY, SOUTHEND.

PERCY RAVEN FOR NEW IDEAS IN COLOURED SHIRTS.

Do not miss seeing his exclusive ranges for 1913.

Number Ninety, High Street, Southend. TELEPHONE 66x.

90, HIGH STREET,
SOUTHEND-ON-SEA,

Dear Sir,

For some time past my Tailoring has been steadily gaining the confidence of City men. I do not profess to compete with the so-called cheap tailors, but guarantee the quality of all goods supplied by me, and gentlemen requiring a tailor where they can feel sure of obtaining a perfect fit and good value for cash are invited to favour me with a trial order.

I have over 500 lengths of cloth to select from, the identical materials sold by West End firms at double the price.

Practical cutter, fitter, and workmen on the premises.

A postcard will bring you patterns.

Yours faithfully,

PERCY RAVEN.

Today Ravens is managed by Neil and Marian Raven and their daughter Hannah.

Clifftown Road 2015

©Barry Edwards

Keddies

Another drapers who witnessed the growth of the High Street in Edwardian times was an ancestor of the Keddie family. Their shop was opened in the 1890s on what was known then as Broadway, developing in a few short years to a large department store. Other drapers bearing the Keddie name opened at Leigh-on-Sea, Hamlet Court Road, Hadleigh and Stratford, but the Southend store was to be the flagship of their company.

Early Family
With Scottish ancestry, a move by George Sim Keddie, born around 1805, established the English branch of the family, when he settled in Hindlesham, Suffolk in the 1840s working as a domestic gardener. Marrying in 1842 to an Anna Reynolds, who was living in the area and quite a few years younger than her husband, they went on to have three children. One of whom Elizabeth Maitland, was named after George's mother who had died when she was young. *"The name Maitland would be given to future generations and in time the name of the building that was home to their department store".* It was to be the last child of George and Anna, George James (1855), who was to be the founder of the drapery empire. Sadly Anna was to die soon after his birth. When George Junior was quite young he travelled up to Scotland, where he served time as an apprentice draper to his father's brother John, who had a drapery business in Auchtermuchty. There in 1871, he had returned to England by 1879, married a Laura Fletcher and settled in Braintree, where he opened a drapers. Remaining there for a good number of years, his wife's, brother Arthur and sister Rosanna living with them. During the 1890s George took the decision to open a drapers in Prittlewell. Taking his sons, Frederick Wallace,

The Broadway Southend 1913

Arthur Maitland and George Douglas with him, Laura and daughter Gladys remained behind in Braintree with her brother, who was also a draper. Taking up residence at 144 Broadway (as the top half of the High Street was known at that time) Laura Keddie rejoined her family, but sadly passed away on the 20th November 1906 and was buried in Sutton Road Cemetery. When the First World War came the Keddie sons like many others were called up. Frederick was a lieutenant in the Royal Flying Core, George Douglas had a commission in the Rifle Brigade in 1915, but in 1917 he asked to be exempt from the war as his brothers had already been conscripted and his father was now an invalid. Request was granted. When George James passed away in March 1921 he left £41,875, granting probate to his sons, Arthur and George listed as co directors of the Keddie business, Frederick named as a draper. He had married in 1915 to an Annie Payne, George Douglas was to marry Hilda Naish a few weeks after his fathers death, Arthur took a wife in 1922, Mary Agnes Blackborrow. Their sister Gladys married Sidney Adams in 1923. Unlike many families who lost relatives during the First World War, George Keddie was to see all three of his sons return home. When Arthur Keddie died in 1954, he was living at The Lawn, Rochford, still owned by the Keddie family. Today it is a wedding and conference venue. In 1986 Murray David Keddie was to be appointed a High Sheriff of Essex.

Keddie Extras

August 19th 1928
At a Southend Court today, Arthur Maitland Fletcher Keddie of The Leas, Hon Secretary of the Southend and County Automobile Association pleaded not guilty to a charge of driving a motor car in a manner dangerous to the public. Result not known.

1939
Mr Wallace Keddie eldest son of Mr Frederick Keddie of Downham Grange, joint director of G J Keddies and Sons, made a fine performance today at St Moritz, in connection with the racing for the converted Curzon Cup on the famous Cresta run.

The Department Store
Within just a few years the Keddies store was an imposing sight on The Broadway which having started at 144 Broadway now occupied a much larger area, from 136–146. Selling everything from penny lines to more expensive items. Extensive advertising in the local papers of the time ensured the public knew what the store offered.

A newspaper report in the 1900s stated, *The growth in the town is perhaps most notable with the rise and development of the well known drapery business of Messrs G J Keddie and Sons of the Broadway. No visitor to the town can fail to be impressed with the row of magnificent shops graced always by wonderful window dressing which for taste and effectiveness is unequalled throughout the county.*

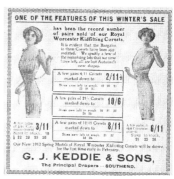
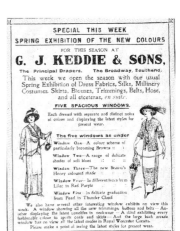

The interior of the department store offering everything a lady could want in the 1900s. There was a household drapery department, linen goods, lino, ladies wear and corsets.

Business has been growing steadily and every year extensions have become necessary. One section was over 2000 sq ft the enabled a separate shop selling household and drapery goods, a further shop sold millinery, mantles (a loose garment worn over indoor clothing–similar to a cape) blouses, ladies and children's outfitters and a corset department. Built on the most modern lines, the shops were well lighted and spacious.

In 1913 Keddies displayed five windows full of millinery, causing a throng of customers to view the displays. This made it difficult for staff to serve all the customers such was the crowd.

In 1934 to rival Selfridges in London they added Palladian pillars to the front of the building and it is this design that those of us who have lived here a long time are most familiar. Another great change came in the 1960s when the family opened the first supermarket in Warrior Square and building Maitland House above it. In the 1980s the store was extensively refitted but by 1996 the company went into administration

High Street

Dixons

Dixons was another well known store in the town for many years. First living and *working in South Norwood, in 1912 John Dixon had taken a trip to Southend on a paddle steamer intending to enjoy only a day out. Having liked what he saw and realising the potential that was available on the burgeoning High Street, he opened a small shop here. Two of his well known shop assistance were the actress Helen Mirrim and Sheila Appleton a local artist, still living locally today.*

Family

Courtesy of Essex Record Office

The Founder of Dixons

John Frederick Dixon 1876–1944 was born in Gainsborough, Lincolnshire the son of a draper/ shopkeeper. His first wife Olive Wadley was a drapers assistant her sister May a milliner, in Croydon in 1911. John Dixon was working in Marylebone at that time, learning his trade in a large department store employing upwards of twenty staff. They married in 1912 and the couple's first child John Francis was born there in 1913. John in latter life would be instrumental in leading the appeal for finance to build what would be called The Dixon Studio (attached to the Palace Theatre).

By the birth of their second child, Olive in 1915 they were living in Southend. Three more children followed, Evelyn 1916, Mary 1918 and Eric Guy in 1921. Daughters Olive and Evelyn married in 1939 to brothers Charles and Donald Foord, their sister Mary married George Johnson in 1943. John Francis the eldest sibling, wed Joan Beech in 1941 with Eric, marrying Margaret McMurtary in 1944. One of their children went on to serve time on Leigh Town Council (Pat Holden) who is still living in the area today. Eric Dixon after reading engineering at Cambridge, joined Marconi's in Chelmsford for fifteen years joining the family firm in 1962 (although he had always been involved in the role of an executive responsible for staff and the building.

Olive Dixon, John Fredericks first wife died in 1937, he remarried in 1941 to a Mary Walsh. Their marriage was short lived as he passed away in 1944, while on holiday at The White Hart Hotel, Gainsborough, Lincolnshire. In his will he left £21,537 16s 4d.

On his death all of Frederick Dixon's children had shares in the business, but John Francis was the managing director. In 1980, when the Palace Theatre wanted to buy the lease of ground just behind its premises, John headed up the appeal to raise funds to enlarge the bar area, provide seating in what was then an open courtyard and to build a multi purpose studio, ultimately known as the Dixon Studio (still very much in use today).

The Store

Coming to Southend in the 1900s was indeed a gamble, as Keddies, Brightwells and Ravens were already here and well established. The Dixon store had started out as several shops in what was the garden of The White House on Cobweb Corner . When the house was demolished in 1936 the Dixon empire expanded by building over the existing shops, a concrete steel and glass building in

Courtesy of Essex Record Office

its place. The department store had now expanded into the high street. The next expansion came after the Theatre De Luxe had burnt down and the department store took over the space. Dixons philosophy was always outstanding value and this was evident from the early days, when underclothing and lace were offered. Later departments sold handbags, baby linen, gloves, hardware, men's fashions and lampshades. In the 1963 they purchased Queens Hall, in Queens Road, using the ground floor first as part of the Jubilee celebrations. The building was not fully renovated and ready for use until 1966, a walkway was built over the road connecting it with the main building. A library run by Foyle's was added and Yardley's offered advice and beauty treatment. There was also a knitting competition, prize £7 with twenty three other prizes. There was free entry for all amateur knitters. Christmas time was special, with the clothes rails being pushed back to make space for a Carol Service for the general public. There was also a top floor grotto for the children. Dixons was the first store to install an escalator outside of London.

1938

77

Don Weatherall
Display Manager
and
Jack Clarkson
a Manager
Courtesy P Holden

Staff Dance Palace Hotel 1938
Courtesy P Holden

John Francis Dixon
P Holden's father
was very musical and
enjoyed the yearly
Christmas Carols

John Frederick Dixon
Courtesy P Holden

The Bridge between the
two stores
© R Dilley

The closure of the department store in 1973, came as a shock to the town. Having received an offer from Hammerson Development Company and knowing members of the succeeding generation were not interested in running the store, they accepted the proposal. For years the company had invested in an independent pension scheme and this would provide pensions for past and present employees. Having traded for sixty years the familiar name of Dixon was to disappear from the high street.

High Street

Sheila Appleton

Sheila Appleton today

A well known local artist with a studio based in the Old Town Leigh-on-Sea painting has always been her first love. In 1945 at the age of 18, she was employed by Dixons, as a shop assistant. Fortunately when John Dixon heard she was attending art college he asked her to become one of his window dressers and also commissioned her very first painting. Although still wanting to be an artist, being a window dresser allowed her to use her artistic talents to create drawings and designs to compliment the goods on display. When Dixon's supplied a canteen for the staff, Sheila was given the freedom to create murals on the walls, to brighten up the area. At Christmas time when the store had a traditional grotto with Father Christmas the opportunity came to produce some magical paintings of fairies and pixies. Later she would create adverts that appeared on the public transport of the day. One was quite unique in that it advertised the installation at Dixons of the very first escalator in the town. Another was telling the public that "Dixons was fighting rising prices".

An early Sheila Appleton painting of customers at Dixons

Staff Party 1950s

A Dixon's fashion Show, Sheila wearing the big black hat

Leaving the store after twelve years Sheila Appleton began to build her reputation as an artist and today many local people (including the author of this book) display her work on their walls. As well as paintings hung in the waiting room of Neil Fraser's Dental Surgery. Today a sprightly 84 year old the work continues at the studio she shares with Richard Baxter.

House Furnishing

Today our homes are filled with fully fitted kitchens, sofa's armchairs and dinning room suites not to mention comfortable bedroom furniture. We are all aware that the rich and landed gentry would employ furniture makers and can still see today the intricate chairs dressing tables and display cabinets they produced. For everyone else they would have to settle for hand me downs or chairs and dressers made by the local carpenter, with the blacksmith making bedsteads which were often covered by straw. A fine example of early furniture can be found in the Heritage Centre Old Leigh. It would be many decades before mass production of furniture within the means of ordinary working people came into being.

Lowe & Hoad

Neville Syer Lowe born Cambridgeshire 1856, he died at Folly Farm, Hockley in 1908, still running the business at 92 High Street.

Edwin Hoad was born in 1855 in London, he died 1936 in Kent.

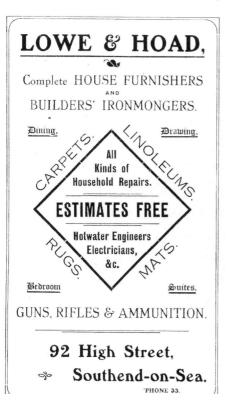

Lowe and Hoad advertised themselves as house furnishers, offering the customer, carpets, bedroom suites, dinning room furniture and all kind of household repairs. What today might seem strange, they also traded in guns, rifles and ammunition. In 1893 they applied for planning permission for additions to the house and shop. Approved.

1910 Green and Son of 68 High Street, would arrange advances for people to buy furniture.

1922 Star Furnishings Company, 84c High Street

Smart and Smart Limited

Smarts was a well know house furnishers on the Broadway (Southend) from the late 1900s. For many years they were offering their services from number 97, but in the 1930s the sons of the founder, Robert Henry Burt Smart had a shop at 93 Southchurch Road and another at 193 High Street. Selling everything for the home, from beds, dinning room suites and chairs fit for the parlour, they offered all that was needed for a working mans home, for just £11.11s. Born in London Robert H B Smart (1868– 1939) was the son of a city porter.

1913

In 1901 Robert worked as an inspector on London tramways and with the tram system becoming quite extensive here, it would have seemed more likely to seek employment with local transport when coming to Southend. Instead by 1910 the move to the seaside had seen a change of occupation to that of a owner of a shop selling all kinds of furniture. With his wife Katherine and daughters Winifred and Catherine and his two sons Robert 1892–1956 and Joseph 1897–1968 he set up home in Southchurch Road. After their father's death the sons continued to run both house furnishers into 1950s.

1913 Newspaper Report
Smart Brothers new premises on the corner of Queens Road and Broadway will have an octagonal tower which at night will be lit by five lights, each of fifty–candle power, shinning through the coloured glass. The building has a frontage of seventy feet to Queens Road and forty feet to the Broadway. The shop

1913

is twenty two feet by sixty six feet and has four large plate glass windows. The lighting is from the ceiling and there is a fine oak stairway leading to the 1st floor, the store will have £10,000 of new stock. The manager is a Mr Harper, the architects are Burles and Harris, the builder Mr H.R. Wilkinson and the shop fronts by a Mr W. Jay who will light them with eight arch lamps.

George Eli Isaac
Manufacturing Confectioner

Son of a packing case maker, George Isaac was born in 1867, following his father's profession in his early years. 1893 he had started his own business as a manufacturing confectioner–sugar and sweets–in Hartington Road (just off the seafront) opening a shop at number 18 High Street, in 1899, where he remained for around fifteen years. Plans were submitted by Isaac to Southend Borough Council to build his factory in Honiton Road also an open shed to the rear of his premises on the High Street. When he died in 1944, his sons Harold and Sidney continued with the business.

Harold Herrett Forge
Restaurateur

FORGE'S Restaurant

25 HIGH STREET
(Few yards Pier and Sea Front)
OUTING PARTY CATERING
WITH PERSONAL SUPERVISION
FOR PARTIES UP TO 120
Lists of Menus on application to:
Proprietor: **H. FORGE**
Tel.: Southend 46345

Harold Forge owned the well known restaurant and snack bar at 25 High Street that stretched back into Alexandra Road. Born in Romford in 1904, he was to join the Royal Navy as a young man and serve on the Ganges 11, leaving the service in 1922. Moving to Southend-on-Sea he married Ivy Robinson in 1927. In 1946 he acquired 25 High Street and ran a car hire firm from that address as well as starting up the snack bar in 1948 (the car hire business closed in 1950) the restaurant lasted until the 1970s. Harold Herrett Forge died in 1974.

Henry Darbyshire
Publisher

Henry Darbyshire, was a publisher and advertising agent who became known for publishing "Darbyshire's Guide to Southend-on-Sea".

Born in Blackrod, Lancashire in 1844 working first as a bookkeeper then moving on to be an advertising agent in his home town in 1881. With wife Emma Kenyon he had settled in Southend by 1891, where he applied to the council for permission to build a shop on the High Street, so he could continue running his business. His booklet was well known around the country for advertising the town and what was available on Southend's seafront in the 1900s. Living on Royal Terrace his wife passed away there in 1915, with Henry Darbyshire dying the following year.

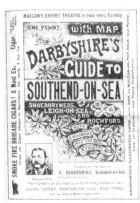

Major Stores

There cannot be many, who have not shopped at any if not all of the following major department stores. So I touch lightly on the subject of each establishment. I can well remember going to Woolworths as a teenager and then later as I grew up. Christmas was a memorable time as I loved to buy my tins of sweets, Christmas crackers and wrapping paper there. I have also been a great fan of British Home Stores, shopping there since the 1960s. My particular favourite is the food hall of Marks and Spencers.

Marks and Spencer

Marks and Spencer today. The store first came to 64 High Street in 1914, but currently its address is 56-64.

Michael Marks a Jewish refugee from Poland, was born in 1863 and came first to Yorkshire where he began buying goods from an Isaac Dewhirst to go out and sell to surrounding villages. This proved successful and he was able to set up business on a trestle table in a Leeds market selling goods for a 1d. Going into partnership with a Thomas Spencer, a cashier with a wholesale firm in 1894, they were to create the world famous Marks and Spencer. Spencer managed the office and warehouse with Marks organising their increasing number of stalls. Eventually they opened their first store and their empire began to grow. Sadly Thomas Spencer died in 1905, Michael Marks 1907 so neither gentleman lived to see the global success of their humble beginnings in Leeds. The business was continued by Simon Marks who in 1911 was a company director and the main breadwinner of the family which consisted of his mother Hannah and four sisters.

Simon Marks introduced the St Michael label and the company were among the first to sell a bra in 1929 and an avocado in 1969.

Thomas Spencer was the son of a journeyman shoe maker from Skipton, Yorkshire. He married late in life (he was 42 years old) to an Agnes Whitfield in 1894. They had one daughter, also called Agnes. Surviving her husband by over 50 years, she was to carry out an enormous amount of charitable work during her lifetime.

High Street

The Woolworth building today 2016

Marks and Spencer came to Southend in 1914 the following businesses were in situ prior to their arrival.

Edwin Smith   Draper
J. Eastman   Bazaar
T.Bowling   Optician

Woolworths

Woolworths as we know was a company started in America by one Frank Winfield Woolworth, but perhaps less well known is the name of William Lawrence Stephenson. When Woolworths decided to open stores in England he appointed W L Stephenson to oversee the project. Realising that importing everything from America would prove to expensive Stephenson was employed from 1909 because of his knowledge of English merchandise. Opening the first store in Liverpool they sold, toys, glass , chinaware, hardware and novelties. It was to be the first of many stores around the country, with Stephenson overseeing much of its growth until he stepped down in 1948. William Stephenson born in Yorkshire in 1880 died in 1963.

F. W. Woolworth & Co.
(Limited)
29-35 HIGH STREET
SOUTHEND-ON-SEA

ROCK, CREST CHINA—Picture Postcards

ICES

CAFE & REFRESHMENT BAR
ON FIRST FLOOR

During the second world war an important notice to all staff was issued

We will continue to pay any member of staff called up to His Majesty's Armed Forces. Existing remuneration inclusive of bonuses will be paid and the individuals service and standing with the company must be maintained.
By order of the board

Southend Woolworths

Opened early in 1914 at 29 High Street, expansion soon followed and they soon occupied numbers 29–31. By the 1950s it had taken over 32–35 and was further enlarged in 1977 with an upper sales floor and even a restaurant. Prior to Woolworths arrival the various sites in the 1900s had been occupied by

Barnet Mendikoff–draper, Frederick Brooks–photographer, Thomas Hills–oyster bar, Going–confectionery, Pattersons–milliners. In 1913 the address of the London Country Bank was numbers 28–30.

High Street

Lift Fatality–Newspaper Report

Pinned beneath the cage of a lift on the premises of F W Woolworths on Wednesday 18th June 1927, was Frederick Biddlescombe aged 16 fatally injured. His back was broken his head badly cut and his left leg fractured.

Frederick had been born in Edmonton Middlesex.

British Home Stores
Another company started by American entrepreneurs who were keen to follow Woolworths example. Modelling their prices and merchandise along the same lines they opened the first store in 1928 in Brixton but didn't arrive here in Southend until 1969. Their address 36–44 High Street. In the 1920s/30s the various businesses were:

36	National Provincial and Union Bank of England Ltd.
36a	Harold Reeve, Dental Surgeon.
38	Victoria Wine Company.
40	(flat) Miss Abbott
40	Gray Bros Grocers
42	Robert Dawson Chemist.
44	William Foot Jewellers.

An added extra of British Home Stores was the grocery department and small cafeterias (the Southend branch offered food in a small sit down restaurant). The business really expanded in the 1930s and by 1960 had 94 stores around the country. In 1986 they merged with Mothercare/Habitat and re-branded itself as simply BHS. The store became famous for its lighting section and good clothes. It has suffered mixed fortune these past few years and unfortunately is now closed.

Astoria

The next few pages are devoted to the cinemas of the High Street but as they have been well documented in Roy Dilley's book "Southend's Palaces of the Silver Screen" I am not writing about them in any great depth.

The Astoria opened in 1935 on the old Luker Brewery site which had been vacant ground for sometime, it was opened by the then Mayor Mr Edwards. A large crowd gathered to see the proceedings. Its short life as the Astoria was not without drama. In 1936 a Mr Albert Cashmore 42 had a heart attack and died during the performance. On a lighter note the election of the 1936 carnival queen, when Miss Francis Haywood was crowned, Edward G Robinson put in an appearance. The following year is was the turn of Miss Evelyn Vaughn a 20 year old waitress from nearby Leigh-on-Sea, to take the crown before a full house. The actor Clive Brooks a film star of note in the 1930s, rewarded her with a kiss. He was famous for having starred opposite Marlene Dietrich in Shanghai Express.

There was serious disruption in April 1938, when the electrical trade union called out its members during a performance. They stopped their projectors, put up the house lights and left the cinema. The organist continued entertaining the audience with popular tunes of the day, while the manager secured other projectionists and the film was resumed.

The cinema was absorbed into the Rank Organisation in 1940 and renamed the Odeon.

Southend Standard

The opening of the Astoria in 1935 saw queues stretching round the building for the first performance which was Brewster's Millions. The star was Jack Buchanan. The site of the cinema had previously been Lukers Brewery

Staff of the Astoria lined up for inspection

Southend Standard

High Street

Odeon

Like many local people I well remember the magnificent building that was the Odeon. Walking into the grand foyer and climbing the sweeping staircase was a wonderful experience. First as a young cinema goer, then in the 1970s taking my young daughters to see Ghostbusters when the audience raised the roof to sing along with the theme tune. I was reminded of the slightly different noise that had been generated on the 9th December 1963, when as a teenager I had attended the Beatles concert at this theatre. Not that I heard the words of a single song for screaming from beginning to end was the order of the day.

Astoria to Odeon

ODEON
IS
AT YOUR SERVICE
IN
SOUTHEND-on-SEA
★
The **ODEON** High Street
OPEN TO THE PUBLIC
WEEKDAYS: 11 a.m. to 10.30 p.m.
SUNDAYS: 7 p.m. to 10 p.m. Doors 6.30
PRICES OF ADMISSION
STALLS: 1/- 1/9 2/3 CIRCLE: 2/3 2/9
CAFE - RESTAURANT
Daily 10.30 a.m. to 8 p.m. Sundays 3 p.m. to 8 p.m.

1947

In 1939 the Astoria was bought by an Oscar Deutsch born in Birmingham to an Hungarian Jew, Leopold Deutsch, a scrap merchant. Ownership of the cinema was brief for Oscar who died in 1940 and the building was taken over by the J Arthur Rank Organisation and re-named the Odeon. Joseph Arthur Rank's family originally came from Yorkshire, with grandfather James Rank, a miller born there in 1829. J Arthur Rank's father, also called Joseph moved to London and was a very successful corn miller, his son born in Hull in 1888 eventually inherited (the company still in evidence today). A devout Methodist, Joseph Arthur was in middle age teaching at Sunday school and producing and showing religious films. Later to combat what many thought was a negative influence, created by so many of the current English and American films, that with a Lady Yule and a young film producer called John Corfield they formed the British National Film Company. So were produced many of the films I viewed while growing up. The Odeon was to enjoy many memorable moments, including the appearance on stage of the great Laurel and Hardy, rock legends Cliff Richards, Roy Orson and Helen Shapiro to name but a few. A landmark occasion was the showing of the first cinemascope movie in the area, The Robe. Several refits took place over the years but the Odeon finally closed in 1997, to be replaced by a multiplex bearing its name at what was Victoria Circus.

© Roy Dilley 1970

Echo Newspapers

Echo Newspapers

**The Beatles who appeared live at the Odeon in 1963 and
some of their screaming fans.**
Permission of the Southend Standard

Arthur Levinson
Echo

A well known manager
Arthur Levinson born in Islington 1925, first came to the Odeon in 1950 where he took up the post of assistant manager, being promoted to manager in 1963. Known as "Mr Entertainment" he is well remembered for organising the 50th Anniversary Night at the cinema. One especially great feat was bringing back twenty former carnival queens for the night. During his time as manager, there would be many rock stars of the 1960s appearing live and notable films shown. He died here in 1990 having enjoyed a long and successful career as manager of the Odeon.

Usherette
Esther Slater was one of many usherettes employed by the Rank organisation. Born in Islington in 1914 to Herbert and Esther Bayliss. Father was a carman. In the 1930s Esther Bayless as she was known then, worked as a maid at the Palace Hotel. In 1940 she married Joseph Slater and eventually settled down in Southend-on-Sea where later she joined the staff at the Odeon.

Garons Cinema

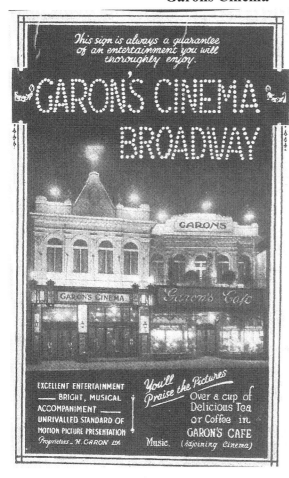

Another cinema of my youth which I used to visit with my friend Katy (still friends today) mainly because the tickets were cheap! When it was built in 1911 it was called the Garons Imperial Bioscope and considered the height of luxury, costing over £5000 to complete. All of this finery was to be overtaken in the late 1930s by new more modern cinemas.

As part of the Garons empire in Southend the cinema was built alongside their cafe, on the site facing Warrior Square. Built by James Flaxman a local builder, who originated from Suffolk had taken up residence in Southchurch in the 1900s with his family. Herbert Crewe an architect from London, drew up the plans. There was a grand opening by the Mayor with musical interludes provided by an orchestra and choral singers and the evening was attended by many local dignities. An Estey organ was added in the 1920s and three ladies Eva, Celesta and Florence Baga were the organists. Living locally they had all been born in London and had been musicians from an early age, following their father Constantine Baga's profession. A ballroom was added above the cinema also in the 1920s and the bioscope was re-named the Garons Cinema. By the 1930s the cinema had undergone alterations and sound equipment was installed. The price of admission remained low making it popular but by 1955 the building was closed and soon demolished

GARON'S BIOSCOPE THEATRE
THE BROADWAY, SOUTHEND-ON-SEA.

Proprietors · · · H. Garon, Ltd. Manager · · · Chas. H. Bowmaker.

ONE WEEK ONLY
COMMENCING MONDAY, FEBRUARY 17th

H. Garon, Ltd. (by request of many patrons, have arranged with MESSRS. GAUMONT for a

RE-PRODUCTION
of a selection of their film of the

LATE CAPTAIN SCOTT'S
SOUTH POLE EXPEDITION

These Pictures will be shown at least FOUR TIMES each day,
in addition to the usual Programme.

CONTINUOUS PERFORMANCE 2.30 to 10.30. ADMISSION 6d., CHILDREN 3d.

NOTE. Intending patrons are strongly advised not to postpone their visit to the end of the week.

Garon's Theatre

To-day, To-morrow & Saturday,
Louise Lovely, Gloria Hope, Carlyle Blackwell
—IN—

The Third Woman

Also Louis Joseph Vance's Novel,
Cynthia of the Minute.

MONDAY NEXT, AND THROUGHOUT THE WEEK.
The Stupendous Film of the Year.

CHARLIE CHAPLIN
With Jackie Coogan
—IN—

THE KID,

A Romance of his own conception. 6 ACTS OF JOY.
It took him a year to make, and it cost him a Million
Dollars, but it's worth every penny and every minute
put into it.

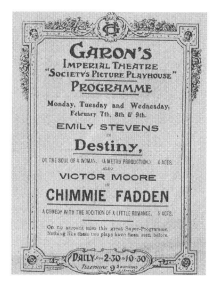

GARON'S
IMPERIAL THEATRE
"SOCIETY'S PICTURE PLAYHOUSE"
PROGRAMME

Monday, Tuesday and Wednesday,
February 7th, 8th & 9th.

EMILY STEVENS
IN
Destiny,

OR THE SOUL OF A WOMAN. (A METRO PRODUCTION) 4 ACTS.
ALSO
VICTOR MOORE
IN
CHIMMIE FADDEN

A COMEDY WITH THE ADDITION OF A LITTLE ROMANCE. 6 ACTS.

On no account miss this great Super-Programme,
Nothing like these two plays have been seen before.

DAILY from 2·30 to 10·30
Telephone 9 Southend.

Theatre De Luxe

The Theatre De Luxe stood on the corner of the High Street with the main part of the building in the London Road. I mention it only because Dixons would expand its store into the space previously occupied by the theatre.

Fire destroyed the cinema on the 8th August 1923. The outbreak occurred around 11pm, after the last performance. The roof soon fully ablaze collapsed and fell in, threatening the drapers store (Dixons) that was next to the building. It was down to the fire brigade's valiant efforts that the store was saved. Although only the cinerma was insured, the contents were not, so the owner a Mr H Kessler was left to bear this loss. The building itself was re-built it was never again a theatre and saw many uses until it was finally demolished in 1936 and then became part of the Dixon drapery store.

The staff outside the theatre Muriel Gratton in the white coat
Permission of G Mee

The Theatre De Luxe was opened in late 1909 and was owned by Electric Theatres. Plans at the Essex Record Office show in 1910, one B Tolhurst (a solicitor at that time in Southend) applying as the owner to build a WC at the De Luxe. An odd thing to own if he was not part of the company who owned the building. Further records show that by 1919 when further plans were submitted for alterations the owners were Theatre De Luxe Ltd. Showing silent low budget films like Pearl White serials. the projector would have been hand cranked.

High Street

Muriel as a young woman
Permission of G Mee

A Member of Staff

For a young Muriel Gratten (born 1902) working at the Theatre De Luxe meant not only helping in the projection room, but playing the organ in the interval. Not surprising that she was musical, for her mother Edith, unusual for the times (1900s) was a professional musician. Her father Ernest Gratten an actor had died in 1909 leaving his widow with three young children, including Muriel.

Meeting with Graham Mee, Muriel's grandson I learnt how after the theatre was burnt down she married and had a family. In later life she became a lifelong member of the Conservative Party hosting many fund raising events. Wanting to see more female representation on the local council, she stood on two occasions for what was then Pier Ward.

Wedding day 20th October 1924 Muriel and Harold Bradley Harvey
Permission of G Mee

PIER WARD

MURIEL HARVEY
Your Conservative Candidate

94

High Street

Salvation Army

The Salvation Army have always been known for good works, but on occasion as these newspaper reports show, they were not always welcome.

September 1894
Prayer for a Sunday trader – Mr John Keith Sykes of Southend High Street was the recipient of a special Salvation Army favour on Sunday last. He was serving Sunday papers outside his shop when suddenly a member of the Salvation Army, a gentleman of good social position, who rejoices in the name of Smith, who was well known upon the stock exchange, walked up to Mr Sykes stall, and kneeling down offered up a prayer. He prayed that the distributor of news might see the error of his ways into which he had fallen. An enormous crowd congregated. Mr Sykes who is a free thinker thanked the man for his attention.

October 1894
Scene in the High Street. For sometime certain traders have been indignant at the holding of evening meetings by the Salvation Army at the High Street end of York Road. On Monday evening as the open air service was in full swing, Mr F J Cumine obtained possession of a horse and trap and by way of practical protest commenced to drive through the gathering of the "army". His passage backwards and forwards among the assembled Salvationists did not greatly disconcert the latter.

November 1897
The Skelton Army. Ernest Garon, son of Frederick Garon – ironmonger, along with a number of others were summoned for wilfully obstructing the free passage of the highway at Southend. Mr T Lamb appeared for the prosecution and Mr F Gregson appeared for Ernest Garon. The prosecution said that on the night of the 10th November there was a procession of the Skelton Army numbering about 500, they had four flags one bearing skull and crossbones. They marched into Alexander Street and halted by the public hall, where they shouted, yelled and hooted at the Salvation Army. Witnesses took away two of the flags from the mob, during the scuffle in which one of the flag poles was broken, the mob was subsequently dispersed by the police. For the defence Mr Gregson called several witnesses who said that Garon neither yelled, hooted nor created any disorder. The other defendants were each fined 5s with 1s 6d costs or seven days in prison.

September 1923
Threats to lynch a motorist in the High Street, were mentioned by the police in a charge of dangerous driving against James Weedon of East Ham whose employer Fred Samson, of Bridge Road, Stratford, was summoned for aiding and abetting him. The car in question, said a constable, in attempting to pass a Salvation Army procession broke it up. The crowd became hostile, mounted the footboard and were threatening to pull Sampson out and lynch him. Samson it appeared was urging Weedon to drive through the crowd, both pleaded guilty. Sampson was fined £10 Weedon £3.

A New Kind of Transport
Trams and Trolley Buses

As Southend became more populated and therefore a busier place to live, the need for transportation became more apparent. Around 1901 the change, although not completely, from horse and cart or carriage saw the introduction of trams. Tracks were laid to Leigh-on-Sea, Southchurch, the Blue Boar, Prittlewell, along the seafront and much later in 1921 track was laid in Warrior Square. The High Street was of course not forgotten, although it presented one difficulty, in that the railway bridge across the street was too low to allow the trams to pass underneath. This form of transport proved so popular particularly during rush hour, that in 1904 it became clear that they were full to bursting and the need for more vehicles paramount. There would be some 65 double deckers and six single decker trams all in the corporation colours of green and cream. The systems hub was the Victoria Circus ticket office, with a clock presented by Mr R A Jones above the building. In 1905 Robert Birkett from Morecombe in Lancashire, was appointed the Borough Electrical Engineer and Tramway Manager. He moved to Kilworth Avenue, Southend, with his wife and four daughters, the youngest born locally in 1907. Boarding with them was another electrical engineer, Arthur Johnson who was born in France. By 1929 Ronald Arthur Fearnley was appointed as Engineer and General Tramway Manager for Southend-on-Sea. Ronald was following in his father's footsteps, as Arthur Fearnley had been the general manager of a local tramways in Yorkshire for over ten years from 1901.

It was surprising how many of the new tram employees in the 1900s came from London but the first three names on the following list were born there.

Charles Frederick Marsh born 1884 was living with his wife Lillian and daughter Mabel born here in 1910, in Albany Road, Westcliff. Worked as a conductor.

Frank Dolby born 1870, died in 1926 still living in the area. His home was North Road, with his wife Edith and son Frank Jnr born Prittlewell 1906. His employment was as a motorman (driver).

James Henry Howe born 1870 died here in 1931. Lived in Southchurch with wife Jane. Another tramway conductor.

Albert Rayner

Albert Edward Rayner born 1878 West Ham, Essex. Another corporation employee (a driver) living on North Road, wife Emma and son Cyril born Southend in 1908, lived with them. The family lived on in Southend-on-Sea until Albert died in 1958 and son Cyril passed away in 1979.

SOUTHEND
CORPORATION TRANSPORT

TRAMCARS

From Warrior Square or Victoria Circus to Leigh-on-Sea, via Westcliff, Chalkwell Park (Sports Ground) and Gardens.
Southchurch.
Kursaal.

From Leigh-on-Sea to
Victoria Circus.
Southchurch.
Kursaal.

TROLLEYBUSES

From Kursaal or Pier to Prittlewell, Eastwood Boulevard and Chalkwell Schools, via High Street, L M S Railway Station, Victoria Circus, L N E Railway Station, Priory Park (museum, sports, gardens and lakes) and Fairfax Drive.
Hamstel Road via High Street, L M S Railway Station, Victoria Circus, L N E Railway Station, Sutton Road (passing Southend Sports Stadium) and North Avenue.

MOTORBUSES

From L M S Railway Station to Sutton Road (Cemetery) via High Street, Victoria Circus, Southchurch Road, Bournemouth Park Road and Eastern Avenue, passing two sports grounds).
From High Street (L M S Railway Station) to Plough Hotel, Westcliff, via High Street, Victoria Circus, Southchurch Road, Sutton Road (passing Southend Sports Stadium), West Street, East Street, Prittlewell, L N E Railway Station, West Street and West Road.
From High Street (L M S Railway Station) to Ness Road, Shoeburyness, via High Street, Pier Hill, Marine Parade, Eastern Esplanade, Thorpe Esplanade and Shoebury Common Road.
From High Street (L M S Railway Station) to Thorpe Bay, via High Street, Southchurch Road, Southchurch Boulevard, Bournes Green and Thorpe Hall Avenue.
From High Street (L M S Railway Station) (winter service) to Eastern Esplanade (Bryant Avenue), via High Street, York Road, Leamington Road (for Southchurch Hall Library and gardens), Woodgrange Drive, Lifstan Way and Shaftesbury Avenue.
From Alexandra Road (for Bandstand and Cliffs (summer service) to Eastern Esplanade (Bryant Avenue), via Alexandra Street, Heygate Avenue, York Road, Leamington Road (for Southchurch Hall Library and gardens), Woodgrange Drive, Lifstan Way and Shaftesbury Avenue.
From Kursaal. Circular tour. During the summer only. Depart from Kursaal every 10 minutes from 10 a.m. to 9 p.m. for a circular tour of the sea front and through the most beautiful boulevards in Great Britain. Fares—Adults 4d., Children 2d.
All routes, with the exception of the Alexandra Road—Eastern Esplanade and the circular tour bus routes, pass through the centre of Southend in close proximity to both railway stations.
Southend Corporation Transport, 95 London Road, Southend-on-Sea.
Telephones: Southend 4487/4488. Telegrams: "Corporation Transport, Southend."

John Albert Lee originally from Worcester was just 18 in 1911 when he was employed by Southend Corporation as a conductor. His father was also employed by the council but as a gardener.

Arthur William Prigg born 1881, Long Melford was employed as a tram driver. 1901 he was boarding with the Barker family and working as a shop assistant. He later married Agnes Barker and they had five children. In 1911 she was living with her family while Arthur was boarding with William Robert Ives—Tram Driver by 1914. Arthur Prigg and family where living in Tudor Road, that same year Prigg was seeking references from the council for other employment.. He died here in 1951.

FIRST WOMAN TRAM DRIVER IN SOUTHEND.

In 1920 the first female tram driver was appointed and was local girl one Annie Overton who married Reginald Sims in 1924.

Southend High Street
1900s

High Street

Trolley Buses

The transport system in and around the town moved from trams to trolley bus between 1925–1928. There were to be 34 trolley buses in operation before they were replaced in 1954 by the kind of transport many of us will remember. One of their drivers was a Henry Sidney How who worked for the bus company during the 1950s The colours for the transport became light blue and cream.

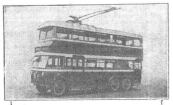

Southend-on-Sea Corporation
Light Railways and Transport
Tele {phone : 6488 {grams : " Transport, Southend."
HEAD OFFICE - 95 LONDON ROAD

VIEW THE TOWN THE BEST WAY
By Trackless and Tramway

TRACKLESS CARS
Run from North to South.
TRAM CARS
from East to West,
all Passing through the Centre of the Town to Many Places of Interest.
"TRAVEL by TRACKLESS and TRAMWAY."

RONALD A. FEARNLEY, A.M.I.A.E., M.Inst.T.,
Engineer and General Manager

1932

Transport outside Dixon's Department store 1950s

Pictured is a Garrett 105 heading towards the Hotel Victoria to enter the High Street.

Southend Corporation, Westcliff-on-Sea Motor Services and Eastern National Omnibus Co Ltd came to an agreement in 1954 for the operation of bus services in an agreed area.

All photographs in this section by kind permission of Middleton Press 01730 813169 further information available in their publications *Southend-on-Sea Tramways and Southend Trolleybuses.*

*Southend Borough Workshop staff working on
pre-World War One open top trams,
providing them with roofs (1922)*

People on Tram.

Track laying in the High Street

Reports In The Newspapers

In the past we would gather our local news from the newspapers and periodicals, today we rely on The Echo and Southend Standard to keep us informed of events and happenings in the High Street and beyond. Has much changed with the decades, from the news items listed below I think not.....

Old News

March 1878 a serious fire broke out at Allan Young's wine and spirit merchants. Attended by the volunteer fire brigade, they finally extinguished the flames, but not before a great quantity of alcohol was destroyed. The fire discovered by Mrs Young, whose husband, being an invalid had to be rescued from the building. Fortunately the premises was insured. Also in attendance to control the crowds gathered to watch was the local police force led by Superintendent Hawtree

Samuel Hawtree born in Hertfordshire in 1835 was the son of a humble carrier. Having risen through the ranks Hawtree served some 31 years in the force, dying at his home in Caulfield Road, Shoeburyness in 1918. A very charitable man throughout his life,

Samuel Hawtree
Permission of Police Museum

he served both the RSPCA and NSPCC and provided a holiday home for the blind.

Two quite contrasting news items were reported in 1882, a fine for contravening bylaws and a serious accident. Edgar White was fined 10s for erecting a building in the High Street without permission of the local board. White was a market trader selling tea. The second more serious item concerned 14 year old Walter Richards from Plaistow who had come down on the train with fellow scholars. Alighting from the carriage whilst still moving, he fell between the platform and the train. Consequently he broke four ribs and crushed one of his feet so badly that it had to be amputated by a local physician, Doctor Jones. While Mary Wingfield wife of a London rope maker, was charged with being drunk and disorderly. Following her husband to the town where he was enjoying a day out with his friends, assaulted him with her umbrella and acted in an aggressive manner towards PC Pryke.

In 1885 a reward was offered to find the person responsible for cutting down a tree on the High Street, without permission.

High Street

Suicide
Susie Sayer, wife of the clothier Charles Sayer of 45 High Street, drowned herself in 1892. Reason unknown. A verdict of temporary insanity was recorded.

March 1900
The deputy mayor heard charges against Alfred Roberts, Charles White, William Boarman, John Gubbins and William Smith of malicious damage. It was alleged that the four men had damaged a plate glass window, the property of a Thomas Offin, by putting their fists through an advertisement case. All were fined, Gubbins £1.2s.0d. Boarman 15s. Smith 17s. and White 17s..
Obviously drink related, these were not young boys but men in their late 30s.

Burglaries
In July of 1900, the newspaper reported that Messer Lowe and Hoad Ironmongers and Mr H Garon general provider on the High Street, had their premises entered but nothing stolen! Mr Drury's shop was not so fortunate as several items were taken. At a meeting with the local police, a Doctor Hopkins pointed out there had been several burglaries of late and extra police supervision was needed.
A familiar cry today.

An item in the paper in July 1904, was a suggestion by the local council to pave the entire High Street with wood! A more serious piece in 1905 was of an accident. George Broom a groom to Mr James Tabour of Rochford (the family still farm there today) was injured when driving along the Broadway, Southend. His horse having fallen breaking the shaft, threw Benson in to the road. Luckily he was only badly shaken. In 1906, skating took place at the pier pavilion (we can only assume as it wasn't stated that it was roller skates) the evening was very successful.

Thomas Dowsett
On the 10th February 1906 the well know JP Thomas Dowsett, was interred in the family vault beneath St Johns Church, of which he was a founder member and a Senior Deacon. The hearse covered in flowers, left his home in Victoria Avenue at 2.30, making its way down the High Street to the town church. The procession that followed consisted of members of the County and Borough Benches, members of the town council and his Worship the Mayor (Alderman Brightwell) with his macebearer.

Thomas Dowset had been a prominent man in the town for many years and would be well remembered.

High Street

Dangerous Driving

William L Wilson, a jobmaster (someone who hires out horses and carriages for family use) was summoned in October 1907 for furiously driving a horse and cart in Southend High Street. Travelling at the rate of 10 to 12 miles an hour, Harry Berrill a storekeeper, said it was a miracle that two children in a perambulator were not killed. Wilson was fined £5 with 10s. costs or face a months hard labour.

A gentleman with the grand sounding name of Alexander Ashmead Hamilton Billamore blew his brains out in Southend High Street in 1908. Aged just 52, Billamore was an underwriter for a British Marine Assurance Co. in London.

Money worries come to mind but Billamore who lived with his wife in St Vincents Road, Southend, left £1236.4s.0d. to his widow Mary.

Serious flooding under the railway bridge 1913
Newspaper Report

In March 1915 a rumour spread around the town that the Midland Railway Company were going to make alterations to their station. This would have involved a number of properties of Garons. The stories proved to be unfounded.

July 1913 a meeting of the Pier Ratepayers Association that the time had come for Southend Corporation to use their influence on the railway with regard to the bridge spanning the High Street. They considered the present construction a disgrace as they felt it was more an ornamental railway bridge.

An unhappy customer in Frederick Smith's, Arcadian Restaurant November 1916, complained that having asked for tea, roll and butter, was served margarine for which he had paid the princely sum of 9d. Summoned to court, the defendant claimed that he bought a mixed butter from a local grocer. However the Chairman Mr J. Burrows stated that restaurant keepers had a duty to their customers to inform them when serving margarine not butter. He was fined 5
Sounds like a modern advert today, I cannot believe its butter.....

High Street

Price Fixing
The well known grocers Schofield and Martin, were fined for selling a tin of sardines for 9d instead of 8d. In their defence solicitor Mr N Mitchell said "Lord Woolton would make as many mistakes as one of the shop assistants if he had to stand for a week in a grocery store". The shop was fined £10 with two guineas costs.
Lord Woolton was a successful department store owner, who would go on to be the chairman of the Conservative Party for 1946-1955.

Explosion
For Gunner Wickham of Shoeburyness, a trip to Southend High Street in 1924 left him shocked and confused, when paving stones were dislodged by an explosion. It was thought to have occurred when an underground cable fused. Wickham was taken to hospital. Another slightly bizarre happening that year, was an incident caused by a shop blind pulled down too low over the pavement. PC Turton patrolling his beat had his helmet knocked off. Donald Munroe, owner, was fined 10s. A fatality on the trams in 1924, when a Mr Edwin Jones of Lord Roberts Avenue died suddenly.

1930s
1932 saw a five minute power failure in the High Street. On the 1st January 1934 a policeman on patrol at 2am, saw a man standing in a doorway of a clothing store. Being suspicious he investigated further, to discover that the man was waiting for the doors to open at 10am, in order to get a bargain for his wife.
There's devotion for you

1935
Mr Beech a travelling salesman had parked his car outside a jewellers in the High Street, when the vehicle went missing. With over £600 worth of samples in the boot, the car which was later recovered in a side street had watches valued at £200 missing. The son of a well known solicitor, William Snow, was arrested in 1937. Henry Snow was arrested and remanded on bail for converting the sum of £363. entrusted to his care by a Percy William Fisher. Mounting the pavement in the High Street, a motorcar knocked down no less that twelve pedestrians, crushed a pram against a shop front and smashed four plate glass windows. Nine of the pedestrians were taken to hospital the driver was among the injured!

Leaflets
On Monday 17th November 1952, leaflets printed in Russian were to be found the entire length of the High Street. The only word to be understood was "Stalin" Police collected up the leaflets which they think were dropped from a passing car. *How strange!*

Living and Working on the High Street

It is not possible to include fully, everyone connected with the High Street, picked at random here are some of the people who simply lived there in the early houses or flats, or were part of the retail experience over the past one hundred years or more. I have taken addresses at random to give examples of how the street changed, from boot-makers, mantle warehouses and drapers, to electrical goods, carpet shops and cinemas. As well as changing retail outlets it is impossible to match all the numbers of the properties with today's postal addresses as there has been so many changes to the buildings over decades.

1800s
Number

10	Jeremiah Poulton Cornell here from the 1850s until his death in 1877. Police Officer.
11	James Clover. Originally from Suffolk died here in 1886 Postmaster.
12	George Raven. Gardener. His wife Mary was a lodging house keeper. One of their lodgers William Harvey was a fireman on the railway.
13	George Keys. Butcher. From nearby Rochford.
14	Andrew Scot. Builders Labourer.
15	James Warner. Bricklayer.
16 and 18	Richard White. A Baker whose shop was at two addresses over the thirty years he was trading.

1850s/60s
Number

21	William Bodgener. Tobacconist.
24	Ephraine Lawton. Came first in 1861 a soda merchant he lodged with a Mr Popelestop from Denmark.
33	William Allen. Stationer, born Poplar 1845. Came around 1870, with wife and one daughter (two sons born here in 1870s) originally a builder living on Cambridge Road. Stayed approximately ten years.
2 and 29	George Attridge. Born in Great Wakering, the son of the local blacksmith, was a gardener working in 1840 for James Heygate at Porters. When he married in 1859 he moved with his wife to the High Street remaining for over thirty years.
32	Hans Peter Holmes. Painter and decorator, born in Denmark in 1819. Moved to Prittlewell in 1868 and married a local girl some thirty years younger two years later. He lived on the High Street for over ten years.

34	James Woodcock. Born Colchester 1834 was a baker. Previously he had owned a confectioners in Ipswich. His father Joseph owned a wood yard.
43	Joseph Packham. Drapers shop.
45	John Tucker. A plumber.
47	Harriett Green. Clothier and hatter. Her son Albert aged 14 was her assistant.
48	James Orbell. Grocer at this address for over ten years.
50	Brightwells.

1900s/1911   **Some of the more unusual businesses/residents**

9	General Steam Navagation Co Ltd
11	New Acreated Beverage and Buffet Co Ltd.
13	Southend-on-Sea Corporation Valuation Department. Richard Weston Hooff was the valuation officer at the time. When he died here in 1961 he was a bank official.
19a	Steam Packet Co Ltd.
29	Artificial teeth maker.
41	Southend Operatic Society.
56	Abbott Bros Milk Contractors.
83	Peter Trigg Office Jobmaster
85a	Seaside Mission
86	Wilson Cycle Works.
100	Metropolitan Academy of Music.

1912/1916

7	S Goldstein Mantle Department.
19	Photographers
22	Maypole Dairy. The business originated in Wolverhampton. Ownership a George Watson from Birmingham.
23	Old Hornchurch Brewery
26	Reginald Ramuz. Solicitor.
28/30	London County and Westminster Bank.
33	P Fonsa. Confectioner.
37	Drapers. Robert Saville born London 1886. His father had a drapers shop in West Ham before moving his business to York Road in the 1890s. Robert opened his own drapers in the High Street in 1913.
39	Parcel Receiving Office.

41/43	Southend and Westcliff Graphic Newspaper.
57	Jewellers – Charles Waller (the son of a provisions merchant) was born in Yorkshire in 1870. His first child was born here in 1898. Having passed the business down through the family there has been a Charles Waller Jewellers on the High Street until the 1960s.
58	Tylers Circulating Library, their advert stated "here you may borrow the latest sixty five novels for 2d per week, Quarterly sub. 2s. 6d. Yearly 9s. 6d."
65	Edwin Smith. Drapers.
67	J Francis and Son. Printer. The business was started by Jabaz Francis in Rochford where he was listed as a journeyman printer. His son Francis followed his father's profession and became a Master Letter Press Printer. His printing works were from around 1890 at 21 High Street. By 1911 he is located in York Road. William Joseph Francis died in 1929. His son Frederick continued as a letter press printer, dying in 1950.
73	Thamesmouth Electrical Co Ltd.
77	Capital Countries Bank Ltd. Manager Andrew Frank Bennie, born in Brighton 1868. His father was a general practitioner who died in 1875. Bennie remained as manager into the 1920s. He died in 1944.
79	Ingram Club.
1920s	
21	National and Provincial Bank of England.
16	Samuel Isaac. Fish Restaurant.
19a	Whatley White. Picture and Fine Art Dealer.
22	Andrew McCarthy. Tobacconist
23	M & S Salmon. Wine and Spirits
25	Joseph Black. Fancy goods dealer
38	Victoria Wine Company.
51	Percy Haywood. Auctioneer.
52a	Mrs Rallings. Tobacconist
57	Charles Waller. Jewellers
71	Ingram Social Club for businessmen. Secretary H L Judd
71a	Isidore Gottschalk Commission Agent (still here in 1933)
84	Star Furnishing Company
86	William A Wilson Motor Engineer
87	Southend-on-Sea Tradesman Mutual Plate Glass Insurance Society. Alfred Whur, Secretary.
90	James Edward Grant. Wholesale Stationers.

104	Goodman Brothers Stationers
126	Alfred Prevost and Son. Land agents/auctioneers/surveyors. A well known family business here from the 1900s. On the High Street for many years passing from father to son, moving to Warrior Square by 1948 where they remained for four decades.
134	A Donntthorne. Baker
145	William Robinson. Fishmonger
152	Miss Edith Overall! Confectioner.
161	Alfred Heeley. Florist
162	World Stores. Grocers and tea dealers.

In 1940 number 38 High Street went up for sale having been in occupation of the Victoria Wine Company for the past forty years. It was described thus:

Ground Floor Shop
Outside yard
1 Sitting Room
Kitchen
Three bedrooms   Price £8200.

Although some of the shops had living accommodation above for the owners of the business below, some were unconnected and simply provided living space to rent. Such was number 122 which consisted of four flats.

1. J Kettley.   2. C Neale   3. T Fitzgibbons 4. A Day

1940s

11	William Forbes. Amusement Arcade
23	Westminster Wine Co
71	Perry and Son Manufacturing Jewellers
122	Brandon's Progressive
132a	J Abbott and Co. Estate Agents
132b	Provident Building Society
132c	Eastman Dyers and Cleaners
132d	Starlight Productions Ltd Theatrical Producers
132e	Betterware Products Brush Manufacturers
148	David Grieg
152	Maypole Dairy Co
154	Westwood's. The Mans Outfitters
162	Renault (Real) Estates Ltd
162	Erac (1946) Camera Co Ltd. Camera Manufacturers
164	Meakers Outfitters

High Street

1950s

2	Martinali Oyster Merchant
8	Goings Fishing Tackle
10	Beverley Hair
12	Nuthalls Restaurant
16	Southend Carpet Co
17	Snowhite Restaurant
19	Hamburger Continental Restaurant
32	Dixons Photographic Studio. The first Dixon Studios were opened in Southend High Street in 1937. The name plucked from a telephone book. Founders were Charles Kalms and Michael Mindel. Things really took off when Stanley Kalms joined the company in 1948 and began advertising in the press.
32a	Lido Restaurant
34	Presto Snack Bar
64	McFisheries
72/74	Lyons and Co
80	Stone Lighting and Radio Specialists
99	W E Sancto. Ticket Writer
153	Southend-on-Sea Masonic Hall Co Ltd
156	British School of Motoring
181/3	International Tea Co
189	Scholfield and Martin.

The first David Greig was opened in Brixton in 1870. By the 1960s there were over 200 shops nationwide. The business was sold in 1972 but continued to trade under the original name.

David Greig was born in Leith Scotland in 1841

Henry Hassell born in 1838 un Middlesex was a pawn broker and clothier (one who makes or sells cloths) at 36 High Street from 1872—1884 when he was the subject of a Receiving Order from the Courts to begin bankruptcy proceedings. After which he moved to London with his large family and was listed as a cigar maker

Henry Hassell

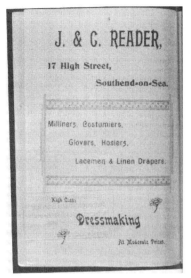

John Montague and Charles Percy Reader. Born in London 1870s. The brothers traded on the High Street for over ten years. Their father was a Silk Storehouse Manager. Adverts 1900s.

Chelmsford Chronicle – Friday 19th May 1911

EXTRAORDINARY SCENE AT A SALE

A bargain sale, "everything marked at 5s.," took place at Messrs. Reader's drapery premises in High Street, Southend, yesterday and caused some remarkable scenes. The shop was advertised to open at 10a.m., but as early as eight o'clock women began to gather in the doorway. As time went on, the crowd filled the entire roadway, and several women fainted. The initial rush led to much destruction of hats and clothing. Ultimately, batches of excited women were admitted from time to time, "full-up" boards being displayed while they occupied the premises.

Underwoods 1928

Edward Carter London 1873. The advert is for 1900. His father was a Licensed Victualler

Alfred John Henry Prevost was born in Stoke Newington London in 1873, His wife Aleida Barerselman whom he married in Prittlewell in 1898 was of Dutch decent. Son Alfred born in 1907 went on to marry and have two sons Anthony 1933, who was later an estate agent and Nigel 1936, a solicitor. Both had offices in Warrior Square.

South East Wine Company
1897

Albert Jennings was born here in 1884, his father William was first a Boot Clicker (a man who cuts the uppers for boots or shoes from leather). His grandfather Samuel was the manger of a shoe factory in the 1870s. Albert Jennings died in 1947 in Rochford leaving £11,074.

Thomas Gilbert, born 1854 Shoreditch
Advert 1898

B & F Tolhurst stood for brothers Bernard and Francis who were both solicitors. Francis lived and practised in Gravesend where the brothers were born. Bernard Wiltshire Tolhurst is more widely remembered here in Southend, Their father Alfred had also been a solicitor, their grandfather Spencer, a bailiff. Bernard W Tolhurst had two sons, of whom one, Bernard Joseph, had been born here in 1891. Like so many families of the time this son was the right age to be enlisted in the First World War, where he died in France in 1917. Retiring to Eastbourne in Kent, Bernard Wiltshire Tolhurst died in 1935, leaving a respectable sum of £162,489.10s.3d.

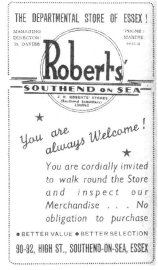

The London County and Westminster Bank was formed in 1913 and opened a number of branches around the country during the First World War.

1936

SAM ISAACS
RESTAURANT
Phone : Southend 6154

Famous for Fish and Grills
Popular Prices

Licensed Lounge and Restaurant
Dancing every evening, Free to Patrons
The Premier House for Party Catering
Seating Accommodation for over 500
persons
Party Tariff on Application

*Centrally situated, in main street, near
Beach, Pier, Bandstand, Kursaal,
Swimming Baths and Stations*

16 HIGH STREET
SOUTHEND

The Company specialises in Seaside Party Catering
Branches at Margate, Brighton, Clacton, also
Hampton Court and Windsor
Party Tariff and full information from Branch
Manager; or General Manager, Nuthalls
(Caterers) Ltd., Victoria House, Vernon Place,
Southampton Row, London, W.C.1

*Serving visitors from 1948 until late
1950s*

A.L. Edwards & Son LTD.
ESTABLISHED 1885

**WHOLESALE TOBACCO MERCHANTS
AND CIGAR IMPORTERS**

Wonderful Display of

**PIPES and
POUCHES,**
**Cigar and
Cigarette Cases,**
Umbrellas,
Walking Sticks
AND
Ladies' Handbags.

70 HIGH STREET,
Southend-on-Sea
AND
20 HAMLET COURT ROAD,
Westcliff.

1920s

*The founder of the bakery around 1905, was Edward Alvin
James but the shops were more commonly known in the
early days as James and Sons. Shops were opened on
Broadway Leigh and Hamlet Court Road. Edward Alvin
James died in 1910, one of his sons Hartley was to die in
1917 of wounds in France. William born 1892 continued
as a baker opening his own shop in Southend High Street
in the 1930s. William Cutler James died in 1965.*

Telephone : Southend 6301.

BROADWAY BAKERY
CO.
WM. JAMES

Artistic Confectioners

※

Winners of Confectionery
Gold Challenge Cup,
10 Championship Cups
and over 300 Medals and
Diplomas.

※

Specialists in Afternoon Tea Fancies

134 HIGH STREET
SOUTHEND-ON-SEA

Mr. W. JAMES

© *James family*

Luigi Offredi first came to this country from his native Italy, he formed a partnership with a Filippo Polti and they managed a wholesale confectioners on the Hackney Road. This partnership was dissolved in 1884, Offredi carried on alone. Married to Emilia they had six children whilst living in Bethnal Green. On coming to Prittlewell they opened a shop on Marine Parade which remained there until the 1880s. His first address on the High Street was number 14, later moving to number 86. During the First World War his business was attacked even though two of his sons were serving in the British Army. Hector in the Machine Gun Corps, and Richard the Royal Fusiliers. The local council paid the Offredis compensation for the damage to their shop. The family continued their business in the town until the 1980s.

Advert 1935

The York Hotel in the 1930s was run by Louis Bertorelli. In 1918 he was a refreshment house keeper before joining up to fight in the First World War. Advert 1935.

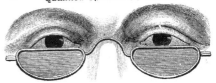
William Charles Day was born in London 1856
and worked first as an Insurance Manager in
West Ham. He died here in 1940 three years
after his wife Emily.

A. WIXLEY & SONS,

SOME OF OUR SPECIALITIES

New and Secondhand Diamond and Gem Rings.

Silver Plate.   Toilet Silver.

Keyless English Lever Watches from 19/6 each,
Guaranteed 10 Years.

REPAIRS OF ALL KINDS DONE In our own Workshop.

The High-Class Jewellers, BROADWAY, SOUTHEND.

Walter Henry James Wixley was born in 1877 in Clerkenwell in London. 1901 he was the manager of a jewellers in the city, living in a boarding house with his brother William who was a mechanical engineer. He was on Southend High Street from 1908 as a silversmith and watchmaker. His son was to take over the store for a few years. Walter Wixley died here in 1959.

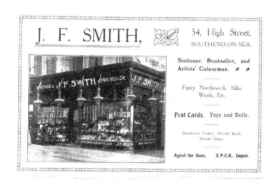

J. F. SMITH, 54, High Street, SOUTHEND-ON-SEA.

Stationer, Bookseller, and Artists' Colourman.

Fancy Needlework, Silks, Wools, Etc.

Post Cards. Toys and Dolls.

Christmas Cards, Banner Bars, White Bags.

Agent for Goss.   S.P.C.K. Depot.

James Frederick Smith born 1855 at St Pancras and his wife Sussanah opened their shop on the High Street in 1890 until the early 1900s. They were living at 8 Dowset Avenue when they died in 1934 and 1935 respectively. The couple had no children

CORPORATION INQUIRY BUREAU, SITUATE AT THE SOUTHERN END OF HIGH STREET AND JUNCTION OF PIER HILL, SHOWING COUNTER AND STREET MAPS. 60,000 ENQUIRIES ARE DEALT WITH HERE EACH YEAR.

Red Buses : 6 from Westcliff, 17 from Eastwood, and Green Buses from Shoeburyness and Thorpe Bay, pass the Bureau every few minutes.

Advertising the benefits of the sea air at Southend-on-Sea

High Street

Victor Silvester
1900-1978

Born in Wembely in 1900 to a man of the cloth (vicar) John Silvester, Victor Malborough Silvester attended the St John's Foundation School for the sons of poor clergyman. When the First World War came he served in the British Red Cross Society and Order of St John and was awarded the British War Medal and Victory Medal. After the war ended he became interested in dance, winning a national dancing competition in 1922, a few months later he married his dance partner Dorothy Newton. Their son Victor Silvester Junior was born in 1924. Opening a dance academy in London it grew into a chain of dance studios across the country, including one above the Odeon at Southend-on-Sea. The 1950s would see him with his own televised series of dance programmes on the BBC. Later he would be appointed the President of The Imperial Society of Teachers of Dancing. The era of ballroom dancing reached its peak when "Come Dancing" was watched by thousands on their TV's. Not only marvelling at the expertise of the dancers, but admiring the wonderful ball gowns worn by the ladies. By the late 1960s rock and roll was beginning to influence the young and change the way they met and danced, but there are still many couples who met whilst dancing at one of Victor Silvester's studios.

Victor Silvester was the subject of This is Your Life in 1957. In 1961 he was appointed The Order of the British Empire. Dying whilst on holiday in France in 1978, his son carried on the Silvester name by conducting his father's orchestra for many years after his father's death.

Victor Silvester Jnr, Tony Wright, Actor and Victor Silvester
Courtesy of Margaret Connon

Margaret Connon

Fellow & Examiner

When just in her teens Margaret Connon developed a love of dancing and went through the medal test system when a pupil at a dancing school. When she was just 17, Len and Edna Wall who were her dance instructors, closed their studio to join Victor Silvester, who at that time was advertising for teachers. Deciding that the world of dance was what she wanted to do with her life, joined the organisation as well, as a trainee teacher. Having entered into a partnership with the Rank Organisation there would eventually be twenty three studios across the country. Her first placement was at the Gaumont State West London, but as new studios opened Margaret was to be sent to Worcester, Kent and Gateshead. In the 1950s she came to the new Victor Silvester studios above the Odeon in Southend High Street.

Margaret and dance partner Peter Billett
Courtesy of M Connon

THE RANK ORGANISATION
High Street Southend-on-sea Essex Telephone Southend 42700

TOP RANK RENDEZVOUS
for dancing

Top Rank
Victor Silvester Studios
Odeon Theatre, High Street, Southend-on-Sea
Telephone : Southend 42700

Letterheads courtesy of M Connon

High Street

Dance Studio

Margaret dressed as a bride for a publicity stunt at the Odeon for the forthcoming film "It Started With a Kiss" staring Debbie Reynolds, Glen Ford and Eva Gabor 1960

Arriving in 1959 Margaret was to be co-principle with fellow dancer Paul Brix, an association that was to last the fifteen years at Victor Silvesters and to see Paul his wife and Margaret forming their own dance school. P & M Studio's in Victoria Avenue, Southend. Paul Brix died in 2005. "When I first arrived the size of the classes were huge, often as many as two hundred eager would be dancers" But Margaret also recalled the number of times people came just to learn the basics to get them through the firms annual dinner dance. The studio was also involved with Southend Carnival, as it was important the current Queen could dance when attending the many events throughout their year in office. "To cope with changing trends, on a Saturday night we had a beat group for the youngsters and they would queue round the block to be sure of getting in". As well as dancing lessons and demonstrations there were Christmas parties and New Year celebrations, "wonderful times" recalled Margaret "we had paper hats, balloons and lots of fun". There must be many couples who met and subsequently married after meeting at Victor Silvesters. When I asked if there were any significant moments she could recall, Margaret replied "there were so many happy memories including when Ella Fitzgearld appeared at the Odeon and borrowed my ironing board and another when she asked me to take part in a publicity stunt for the cinema".

All good things come to an end and with changing tastes, in the late 1970s the Victor Silvester Studio in Southend High Street became a bingo hall. Moving on first to the Ritz cinema then for a time classes were held at the Royal Stores. With the formation of their own dance studio (still there today) Margaret travels the country and indeed the world as a qualified examiner.

Margaret Connon today 2016 still very much involved with dancing. Travelling all over the UK and the world.

Ray Woodcock

There must be many couples who met at Victor Silvester's studio here in Southend. One such person was Ray Woodcock, who met and married his now ex–wife Carol in 1968. His first visit to the dance studio with a crowd of friends one evening he in his own words was quite disruptive on the dance floor. One of the instructors Paul Brix must have seen potential in the young Ray, for he persuaded him to take ballroom dancing a little more seriously. In time he studied and passed the various grades, he began teaching the dances of the day. Waltz, foxtrot rumba, quickstep. cha cha cha all the dances so familiar to our parents. "We closed at was then considered quite late around 10.30 but when disco came in it was not unusual for them to close around midnight". Ray recalled how a number of people would come in about a week before a special event "they would be pleading to be taught the basics of the waltz or quickstep so they could survive the firms annual dance." Ray concluded with saying what a happy time it had been and he had met a lot of lovely people on the dance floor

1970s

Photos © Evening Echo

One of the many Christmas parties held at the studio in the 1960s.

Photos from the 1960s
© Evening Echo

My thanks to Ray Woodcock for providing these photographs

High Street

The following two pages show the High Street today (2016). Fortunately some of the wonderful architecture above the shops is still there for everyone to see. If you look closely above KFC you can just make out Offord's Café. When next walking down the High Street, look up; to view part of Southend's history, remembering not to collide with people on their mobile phones.

The Royals 2016

All photographs © B Edwards

All photographs © B Edwards

Accident outside the London Hotel 1940s
Courtesy E Wells

Demolition 1950s
© P Wren

Originally Boots the chemist shop
© B Edwards

Once home to Thomas Dowsett
© B Edwards

© R Dilley